*His voice was low but Derry
felt each syllable pulse in her blood . . .*

"Little tiger." Aaron chuckled. "Devil doll."
His mouth closed over hers, marking her as
his, brooking no other opinion. His hands
travelled possessively over her body, the heat
in them warming her from throat to navel.
Derry felt her eyelids heavy on her cheeks as
Aaron rose with her in his arms. She sighed
as the silken sheets on the bed caressed her
back, her arms going up unconsciously to
entwine at his neck. She felt a momentary
rebellion at his ability to control her so
effortlessly, then she spiralled out of conscious
thought, Aaron becoming her only anchor,
her only reality.

WHAT ARE *LOVESWEPT* ROMANCES?

They are stories of true romance and touching emotion. We believe those two very important ingredients are constants in our highly sensual and very believable stories in the *LOVESWEPT* line. Our goal is to give you, the reader, stories of consistently high quality that may sometimes make you laugh, sometimes make you cry, but are always fresh and creative and contain many delightful surprises within their pages.

Most romance fans read an enormous number of books. Those they truly love, they keep. Others may be traded with friends and soon forgotten. We hope that each *LOVESWEPT* romance will be a treasure—a "keeper." We will always try to publish

LOVE STORIES YOU'LL NEVER FORGET
BY AUTHORS YOU'LL ALWAYS REMEMBER

The Editors

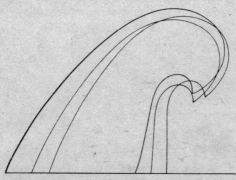

LOVESWEPT · 2

Helen Mittermeyer
Surrender

 BANTAM BOOKS · TORONTO · NEW YORK · LONDON · SYDNEY

SURRENDER
A Bantam Book / May 1983

ISBN 0-553-21604-X

Published simultaneously in the United States and Canada

*Bantam Books are published by Bantam Books, Inc. Its
trademark, consisting of the words "Bantam Books" and the
portrayal of a rooster, is Registered in U.S. Patent and Trademark Office and in other countries. Marca Registrada. Bantam
Books, Inc., 666 Fifth Avenue, New York, New York 10103.*

PRINTED IN THE UNITED STATES OF AMERICA

O   0 9 8 7 6 5 4 3 2 1

One

Derry knew that she would see the giant with the dark blond hair flipped back from his wide forehead. He had been there every day for a week. She had cannoned into him as she had raced for a Psych II class to which she was always late, and he'd swept her high off the ground, laughing into her wide-eyed face.

"Take it easy, little one. You'll get there."

"I'm not little. I'm five-feet-eight and muscular from swimming," she'd mumbled, still suspended in the air, liking the feel of those long, capable hands clasped at her waist.

"You're a tiny angel," he had insisted, bringing her closer to him.

"No. Let me down. I'll be late," Derry had squawked, making the giant laugh. He had released her but told her he would see her again. And he had . . . he'd been there every day for a week.

Yesterday he had asked her out, and she had

said that she would go with him. Now Derry was sure that when she saw him, she would tell him that she wouldn't go with him, that he wasn't to pick her up from the dorm.

She was so shocked not to see him waiting for her at O'Connor Hall that she stood still for a moment, blinking as though she could somehow make him appear. She desperately wanted to see him so she could break the date. Good Lord, she was going out with a man whose name she didn't know!

That night she drove her roommate, Marcy, wild by changing into and out of every outfit that both of them owned.

At exactly seven o'clock he knocked at her door, dressed in beige jeans and a matching jacket, making Derry sigh with relief because he had dressed informally.

He smiled at her as he led her out of the dorm to the low-slung Ferrari that had a crowd of admiring students around it. He answered some questions from the men looking at the car after he'd assisted Derry into the passenger seat. Then he came around and joined her in the elegant cocoon. "I hope you like Japanese cooking."

"I do." Derry turned in her seat to look at him and felt herself redden at the assessing grin he threw her way. "Where are we eating?"

"My place." He threw the Ferrari into gear, shot around a curve and up a ramp to the expressway.

"Hold it," Derry said, one hand going to the door handle. "I thought we were going to eat."

"We are. Take your hand from there and stop imagining I'm the great white slaver your mother warned you about. I have a fantastic cook who specializes in Japanese cooking."

"My brother!" Derry exclaimed, realizing sud-

denly that she didn't even know her date's name and hadn't even introduced him to Marcy.

"What?" His head slewed toward her. "You're a gorgeous brunette, but you're crazy. What do you mean by 'my brother?' "

"It was my brother who warned me about white slavers, not my mother. What's your name?"

The giant roared with laughter, making Derry's lips twitch in an answering smile. "My name is Aaron Lathrop, and it's my construction company doing the work at Laneport."

"Oh, I see. You're a construction worker." Derry leaned back against the soft leather of the seat.

"Among other things. Lathrop Enterprises has its fingers in many pies." His tone was casual, but the glances he threw her were far from offhand.

Just outside the city he turned into the parking lot of a large high-rise apartment building. The Stratford was a very exclusive address, which Derry had never so much as dreamed of visiting. He parked in the underground garage, and they took the swift, silent elevator to an upper floor where only two doors led off a hallway. Aaron unlocked one of them, and they entered an elegantly decorated foyer.

A slim Oriental man waited for them. His black suit echoed the shoe-black color of his hair and the patch he wore over one eye. He smiled broadly at Derry. "Good evening," he said, no trace of an accent accompanying his words. "I was born in California and lost my eye on a racetrack out there. I also have a pin in my right leg and enjoy cooking."

Derry stared at him openmouthed.

Aaron grinned at her and took her arm. "He has atrocious manners, but we went to school together and he knows too much about me, so I can't get rid of him. Derry Parker, meet Jim Sagawa."

Derry felt her shyness melt away in the true warmth of the bonhomie of these men.

"Now," Jim said, "I have to leave you with this bore, beautiful lady. But at least you will enjoy the dinner." He flipped his fingers in a mock salute intended to make Derry laugh, and it did.

"Don't encourage him," Aaron whispered, his breath feathering her ear. "Ummmm, you smell good."

"Thank you." Derry gulped, moving away. "It's Shalimar. My brother gave it to me."

"You seem close to your brother." Aaron led her to the living room where an oaken bar laden with bottles was spot-lighted by a ceiling lamp. "What would you like to drink?"

"Ah . . . I . . . a Manhattan, please." Derry hoped that would be a palatable drink. She couldn't think of any other cocktail.

Aaron stared at her for a moment. "Are you sure?"

Derry nodded once. "Yes."

Aaron mixed the drink. "I can't say I'm partial to Manhattans." His brows rose as he handed her the glass. "I hope it's the way you like it."

Derry smiled and lifted her drink. "Cheers." She took a swallow of the coffee-colored liquid and coughed, feeling her eyes water. "Good," she said huskily, blinking several times.

Aaron turned away, smiling. He poured whiskey over ice, and Derry seated herself on one of the white overstuffed sofas that formed a horseshoe in front of the fireplace. She admired the room's cool colors and tasteful furnishings. The steel blue tones in the fieldstones of the fireplace were echoed in the wall to wall carpet and a plush chair. Aaron joined her on the sofa. His gaze was intense, and his hand circled slowly, swirling the dark liquid over the ice in the glass. "I prefer Irish if I drink whiskey. Other times I drink beer, a holdover from my college days."

"Oh. Where did you go to school?"

"Harvard."

"Oh."

Silence fell between them then; Derry could think of nothing to say and grew uncomfortable. She sighed with relief when Jim announced that dinner was ready. But she almost groaned when, just as they were seated at the dining room table, he indicated that he was leaving.

"Nice meeting you, Derry." Jim waved and left quickly.

"Don't be so nervous, Derry," Aaron said. "I'm not going to jump your bones." He passed the steaming vegetables to her and forked thin slices of tenderloin and succulent prawns onto her plate.

All during dinner Derry cursed herself for her stupidity as she complimented the food and remarked on the weather. She could never remember feeling so gauche or awkward. They took their cups of fragrant tea into the living room, and when Aaron put his down and turned to her, she jumped.

"Stop it, Derry." He leaned over and let his hands run down the anthracite curtain of her hair. "I'm not going to rape you. Rape is an act of a sick mind. I assure you I don't qualify." He inhaled, his face closer now. "Your hair smells so good. So does the rest of you."

"Thank you." Derry turned her head toward his, not realizing their faces would be only inches apart. She stared into Aaron's sea green eyes and suddenly felt motion sickness. "Oh."

"Oh, yourself, devil doll," he whispered, his breath tickling her lips. "You are beautiful."

"Thank you." Derry gulped as she felt her body being pulled close to his.

"And polite, too." Aaron's mouth pressed lightly against hers, his lips brushing back and forth. The rhythm increased in slow, warm cadence.

All at once Derry felt untethered. Reason intruded, and she lifted her head. "Do you like music?" she asked.

Aaron chuckled. "Yes." He lifted his arm and reached behind the sofa. "How about some Linda Ronstadt?"

"Like it." She felt her skin prickle as their breath mingled.

Throaty love words filled the air around them, but Derry could not have said what song it was. She only knew she loved the aura she was in with Aaron.

"I told you that I wouldn't rape you and I meant it," Aaron said in a low, firm tone. "But that doesn't mean that I won't try to make love to you." The tiny bites he inflicted on her neck had Derry's blood galloping through her veins.

She pushed back from him weakly. "Then I don't suppose you'd believe the one about not kissing on the first date," she muttered, her fingers running up the side of his face and down again.

Aaron grinned at her, his hand working at the top button on her Indian-cotton dress. "I'm glad to hear that, but I don't think you'll have that problem ever again."

"No?" Derry asked weakly, loving the feel of his hand at her breast as he undid the rest of her buttons.

"No," Aaron muttered, "you won't be going out with anyone else again, not ever." His words were slightly slurred. He carefully parted the dress and slid it over her shoulders. Her arms glided free of the sleeves. Aaron's eyes fixed on her body, naked to him from the waist up. "No one is ever going to look at this but me." His gaze rose to her face, his eyes seemed to deepen to a shade of forest green. "I want to make love to you now, Derry, but you're young. I'll give you more time, but not much more." The red staining his neck crept up his cheekbones as he continued to stare longingly at her.

Derry was shocked at the response of her body to his look: her nipples hardening; her breasts filling and swelling. "Aaron?" She reached out for him. "I don't need any more time." The words coming out of her mouth surprised her almost as much as they did him. She, who had always been somewhat indifferent to the panting and petting of the boys she dated, now throbbed with desire. She wanted to experience all the things her floormates giggled and whispered about, and she wanted to experience them with this man.

"No, devil doll, not this time," Aaron whispered against her mouth. "I want it, too, but we'll wait."

"Who died and left you boss?" Derry growled, nibbling at his lower lip, feeling childish and queenly all at once.

Aaron laughed at her, but Derry heard the quaver in his voice and felt a surge of womanly power. He was on his feet with her in his arms before she could say more. "I'm taking you home, little one. We'll have dinner here tomorrow night."

Derry was confident that Aaron would make love to her the next night. He didn't. Instead he seemed to be more withdrawn from her. She was sure she wouldn't see him again as he walked her to the dorm security doors. But then he gave her a hard, openmouthed kiss and muttered, "Tomorrow night." He stepped back, spun on his heel, and strode toward the Ferrari. He'd left the motor running and the headlights on.

The fifth night they went out was a Friday, and

Derry was in love with Aaron. She had difficulty eating and sleeping when she was away from him. It seemed to her that nothing worked smoothly. Her walk seemed jerky, her arm movements ungainly—even her complexion seemed sallow when she wasn't with Aaron. One of her classes met in a room that overlooked the construction site of the complex that Aaron was building in Laneport. That classroom was soothing because there she was closer to some things that belonged to Aaron: his big, earth-moving machines, his workers.

Marcy and the other girls on the floor had already left for the student union when Derry began to dress for her dinner date with Aaron. Most of her friends had stopped asking her what she was doing in the evening, since her answer had been the same five times.

She pulled out a black silk dress that her parents and her brother, Dev, had purchased for her in New York. Oh, she and her sister-in-law Sandy had been there, but Dev and their parents had done all the talking and deciding until Sandy had reached out and grasped the dress with the satin underslip and one bare shoulder. Her father and mother had frowned, but Dev had listened to Sandy when she had described Derry as mature, attractive, and sophisticated enough for this dress. Dev's eyebrows had arched when Derry had modeled it, turning so that the inverted pleats fanned open halfway up the skirt, emphasizing her long legs. The top delineated her rounded breasts and small waist.

Now she looked at herself in the narrow closet mirror and scrutinized her tall, slender body. Her uptilted breasts were outlined quite clearly in the black silk. The breasts were all right, she conceded as she twirled in front of the mirror, but it would help if her rear weren't quite so rounded.

The black silk seemed to emphasize it, and she moaned to herself. But she smiled at the length of her legs. Her ankles seemed almost fragile in the high-heeled, black leather sandals, which were the only good evening shoes she owned. She twirled again, feeling very feminine without the flat shoes she usually wore for her dates. She put her hands to her hot cheeks, thinking of Aaron's six-feet-three-inch height, and how she had asked him how tall he was right away. She closed her eyes as she thought of the width of his shoulders, his strong thighs, the muscular arms that had lifted her.

When she heard Aaron's knock on the door, she took deep breaths to steady herself before grasping the handle and turning it.

Aaron was silent so long, his casual stance against the jamb unchanging, that Derry felt nervous. He straightened slowly, his eyes still narrowed on her. "Ready? I thought we would eat out this evening, so it's fortunate you dressed up."

"Isn't it?" Derry's voice had a hollow ring. As he draped her coat over her shoulders, disappointment swelled in her.

They drove to a country club where Cadillacs, Lincolns and even a couple of Rolls Royces filled the parking lot. Aaron spoke with easy familiarity to many of the people—from the parking attendants to fellow guests—but he introduced Derry to only a few of them. She felt too miserable to enjoy the Seafood Pasilico Aaron ordered for them, and the white wine seemed too sharp to her. She was glad to forego dessert and to have only coffee. Tonight would be the last night she would see Aaron! It was stupid to be so madly attracted to—no, head over heels in love with—a man who ignored you most of the evening.

She marched ahead of him out the door to the

club, anger and pain adding speed to her movements.

"Slow down, angel." Aaron took her elbow, crooning to her.

"Make up your mind," she snapped, standing next to the car but not looking at him. "Either I'm an angel or a devil. I can't be both."

"You can be, and you are," he said with authority. Then he eased her into the car and went around the front to his side. He pushed back from the steering wheel and looked at her intently. "Tell me why you're so angry with me."

"I want to go back to the dorm, please." Derry's voice sounded too loud and shrill in the opulent confines of the small car.

Aaron stared at her averted profile for long moments, then shrugged, turned back, and started the engine. He drove onto a picturesque side road that meandered through the rolling hills of the golf course. "Talk to me."

"No." Derry curled her hands into fists. She could pummel him for not loving her! She could throw him down a well, out of an airplane, off a building. She was so engrossed in her bloodthirsty thoughts that she didn't notice they had gone past the college turnoff. The sudden darkness made her realize that they were in the underground garage of Aaron's apartment building. She straightened. "What are you doing? Take me back to the dorm!"

"I will . . . as soon as you tell me what's bothering you." He opened her door and looked down at her. "Now do you get out or do I lift you out of there?"

"I can sit right here and tell you why I'm angry. I don't need to get out of the car." She could feel her lower lip jutting forward.

"Derry," Aaron hissed, reaching for her.

"Okay, Okay, I'll get out, but we'll be coming right back down again." She tore at the fingers he had clasped around her upper arm, trying to pry them away. "Stop it. I can't walk this way. I feel as though one side of my body is longer than the other. Aaron, let me go." She panted as he pulled her into the elevator. She turned around to tongue-lash him and felt herself being folded against his body. His mouth came at hers like a missile. Her body shifted downward into passing gear, blood sizzling through her veins, her heart-beat way over the speed limit. His kisses made her feel as though her insides would burst through her skin. With the sudden lifting of his head her body sagged and only his arms kept her from falling.

"I'll never let you go." Aaron looked down at her, his voice curiously bland. He led her from the elevator. "We'll see what's in the refrigerator. You didn't touch your dinner."

"Jim won't want you in his kitchen." Derry licked her desert-dry lips.

"Jim's in California visiting his family. They moved from Boston because Jim's dad has very bad asthma."

"Oh." Derry rubbed her arm when Aaron released her to look into the refrigerator. "He should have come to New York State. We have lovely, clean air."

Aaron lifted his head and winked at her. "Ah, yes, the sleet, snow and gray days are so salubrious."

Derry inhaled deeply. "Don't you mock my state you Massachusett . . . ah, Massachusetta . . . ah . . . whatever they call you people."

"Bostonians." Aaron bit into an apple.

Derry glared at him, then reached past him for an apple for herself. She watched Aaron put on the coffee and then switch the machine to automatic brew. She glowered at him as he sliced homemade bread. When he would have reached for a package of sliced ham, she reached past him again and pulled a jar from the refrigerator.

"I like strawberry jam."

They sat at the kitchen table while Derry ate a sandwich and Aaron ate another apple and they both had coffee.

Aaron wouldn't let her wash the dishes, saying he would stack them in the dishwasher. "We're having a liqueur and you're going to tell me why you were mad at me." He pulled her after him into the living room. He put a taper to the fire already laid in the stone fireplace and poured liqueurs for them, then sat down next to her on the sofa. With one strong arm, he folded Derry next to his body. "Now tell me," he said. His breath was hot against her forehead. "What's wrong?"

Derry had every intention of telling him to go straight to hell. "You ignore me," she blurted, feeling heat in her face, furious at how gauche she was with this man. "I'm not going out with you again." The angry statement made her feel better and more rotten at the same time.

Aaron drew a deep breath, taking the tiny crystal liqueur glass from her fingers and letting it join his on the table in front of the sofa. "I'm not ignoring you, angel. I'm trying to exercise a little control where you're concerned." His hand lifted her chin and he leaned back so that he could see into her eyes. "You're very young, and I don't want to hurt you."

Her body bloomed with relief, and she reached out her hand. Her long nail trailed down his cheek. "You hurt me when you ignore me."

"Derry, I told you that I haven't . . ."

"Kiss me, Aaron." Derry feathered her hand around his ear and down his neck. She watched the muscle in his neck jump, her fingers sliding to the spot and pressing, the pulse beat going into her body and becoming part of her. She smiled up at him, her eyes half closed, feeling as though her lashes had taken on the weight of lead.

"God, help me!" Aaron's mouth came down to fasten on her parted lips, the thrust of her tongue going in search of his. He withdrew enough to mutter, "Derry, darling . . . don't . . . no . . ."

"Yes," she said hotly. She unbuttoned his shirt and ran her fingers over his chest. She played with the coarsened curl of hair past his belt buckle. It surprised Derry when she felt an urgent desire to see him without his clothes. She had never thought she would think a man beautiful, but after she pushed the shirt from Aaron's shoulders and watched the play of muscles under the taut, tanned skin, she spoke her thought. "You're gorgeous." She could feel her eyes widening as she watched the run of color up Aaron's neck and into his face.

"You don't call a man gorgeous." He chuckled, and one hand came up to cup her face.

"Do you know the effect you're having on me, devil doll? Do you know what your words do to my insides?" His voice seared her face. "Don't." His hands went to his belt as Derry struggled with the buckle. "Derry, you're so young. We should wait until you finish your education."

"This won't interfere with my education." Derry laughed, coming up on her knees on the sofa and leaning over Aaron as she pressed him back into the cushions. "It might even stimulate my intellectual activity." She nipped at his chin with her teeth as his hands came up and clutched convulsively around her waist. "Unless, of course, you would like me to gain some useful experience at Laneport with someone else before I tackle the great Aaron . . ." The room spun around her as Aaron heaved her up into his arms and then placed her flat on her back. He bent over her.

"Don't say that," he warned, his voice harsh. "*I'll* be your only experience."

"Good. I'm ready." She reached up and pulled his head down to her, forestalling the protest she saw forming on his lips.

Her confident aggression turned Aaron into fire. He groaned her name against her mouth.

Derry felt her body lifted upward into the curve of his as Aaron took charge of the loving. She sensed an angry helplessness in him as his hands burned a path up her body and down again. The desire to destroy what little control he had left, drove Derry to nip at his shoulder, to rake her nails down his back.

"Derry . . . Derry. My God." Aaron clasped her body to him and lifted them both from the couch with one powerful surge of muscle.

Derry watched the white face so close to her own as he carried her into the bedroom and placed her on the king-sized bed covered in black alpaca, the sheets and pillowcases a clotted cream color. Before Aaron followed her down to the bed, he finished removing his clothing. Trousers, belt and shorts were flung into a heap. His face seemed as though it was carved from ivory, his tanned skin having a saffron cast as he looked down on her. He knelt on the bed beside her, his naked body gleaming in the light from the small bedside lamp. "I'm going to undress you, my devil doll." He bent over her, his words slurred. "First I'm going to get rid of this dress that's been driving me crazy all evening." He lifted it over her head with little fuss, holding her free of the bed with one hand. "And your slip, and your panty hose, and . . ." Aaron stared down at her body clad only in the peach-colored silky briefs, the silence throbbing between them.

Derry watched him, a happy nervousness pervading her. She didn't want to disappoint Aaron, but she felt no trepidation in giving herself to him. She was impatient for him. "Aaron?" She tried to bring him back from the deep study of her body. She wanted him close to her.

"Ummm?" His eyes flicked to her face, a muscle moving in his jaw. "You're so damned beautiful, Derry—and now you're mine." He moved down over her again, the sureness of his motions telegraphing his decision that there was to be no more holding back.

His hands were gentle on her but forceful as he strove in tender fashion to bring her body to a white heat. She was on fire for him long before he began the gentle entry into her body and past the sharp pain to begin the rhythm of ecstasy which caught them both. Derry felt as though her skin had melted into her flesh and that her flesh had melted into Aaron's. Her slippery hands slid down his body as she attempted to hold him closer. She heard a hoarse voice call out his name, and was startled to discover it was her own. Derry never wanted the hot spiral to end and when Aaron's body shuddered over hers at last, her own answered with a wild and wonderful explosion of quaking.

"I love you, Derry," she heard him whisper, and contentment spilled through her. "We'll marry right away." That shocked her so that her eyes flew open.

"We don't have to marry," she whispered through cardboard lips.

"Oh yes we do, devil doll, and don't try to get out of it." He leaned on one elbow, his eyes travelling in restless heat over her body. "Don't you want to marry me?"

"Oh, yes. But I'm still in school."

"You'll stay in school at Laneport. I'll arrange my work schedule so that we can live in this area until you graduate." His hand traveled down her cheek to her neck. "Did I hurt you, my angel?"

"For a moment." She grinned at him, pulling his head down to her so that their faces were inches apart. "Most of it I liked very much." She nibbled on his earlobe before gently pushing him away to study his expression. "So that's what all the girls have been raving about!" She giggled, feeling his muscles tauten on her body. "I should have tried it sooner."

"No," he growled, his hands clenching on her, the smile on his lips belied by the glitter of his eyes. "You've had your first and last man, my angel." His tongue licked along her jawbone. "Oh your experiences in love making will continue to become more varied and interesting but your partner will always be me."

"Bossy." Derry laughed but she felt a niggling of resentment that Aaron felt he had to be so positive with her.

"I love your body." He bent over her, taking a rosy nipple into his mouth.

"I sensed that." Derry gasped, her body pressed back into the pillows on the bed.

"Smart girl," Aaron muttered, his mouth moving down to her navel. "It's nice to know you're benefiting from a college education." His voice had a guttural sound as his mouth continued to caress her body.

"This is an education?" Derry stuttered.

"The best one you'll ever have. You are going to spend the next sixty years doing this, so I think sound, basic elementary education is important." His tongue ran over her instep, making her foot jerk in delight.

"I didn't know feet were erotic." She was drowning again.

"Every pore on your body is erotic, angel mine." Aaron breathed the last words into her mouth as his body shuddered with sudden need.

There was no time or space for them again as they created their own, inviolate world. Aaron teased and cajoled, restraining himself, as he brought her to the edge time and again.

"Aaron, please! Please, Aaron!"

"Yes, my devil doll. Yes!"

Derry awoke to the sound of the children crying, her own body bathed in perspiration, tears streaming down her face. The children's nightmare had awakened her from the dream again. Ever since their arrival over a month ago, the three children had had the recurring nightmare about losing their parents . . . and more and more often Derry had dreamed of Aaron.

"No, no, no." She struggled into her robe, sniffling. "I will not let that man invade my dreams, my life." She staggered down the hallway, calling to the children. "It's all right. I'm coming. I'm coming."

I will protect them and care for them. I will. I will, she swore to herself, hugging the three shivering children close to her own trembling body. "It's all right. We're together now. We're a family."

I'm a twenty-seven-year-old woman, not a naive eighteen-year-old. I can and will take care of this family, she vowed, holding the children closer.

Two

Derry sat with her hands twisted together, listening to the lawyer, Wilson Chambers, tell her that her brother and sister-in-law had left her in sole custodial control of their three children and a small trust fund. She sighed, nodding, knowing beforehand what the will would say, for she, Dev, and Sandy had discussed it before it was written. Now the reading of it brought home to her with great force that she would never have the comfort and love of her brother and sister-in-law again.

She blinked when Wilson spoke to her. "Yes, I'm fine." But I'm also remembering that less than a month ago you told me that my divorce from Aaron was final, she thought in numb acceptance, that you urged me to accept the generous alimony Aaron provided, that you were upset with me when I wouldn't. She stared at the man who looked at her with concern. How *could* you think I could take money from him? It would seem like a payoff for our married years. She had been sure that day that she would never marry again when she and Aaron parted after the decree. Now, six months later, she knew that marriage was something she might have to consider . . . but not to Aaron. She hadn't seen him for six months.

She shook her head to clear her thoughts. "Do you think the children are all right in the waiting room?" She knew her smile was stiff as plastic.

"Of course, Derry. Mrs. Schultz is very motherly."

She nodded, lifting the will from her lap. "It says here that Dev prefers that the children be raised in Laneport and not in the city?" At Wilson's nod, she took a deep breath and thought of Gerard's proposal. She had fully intended to refuse him. She was fond of Gerard Holden, even mildly stimulated by him. She preferred that to the volcanic relationship she had had with Aaron.

She shook her head again, not wanting to think of Aaron.

"Of course it will be difficult for you, raising three young children all by yourself." Wilson coughed, his spaniel eyes full of sympathy. "And these children were very close to their parents." He cleared his throat, wiped his glasses, and smiled at her. "Do you think you will be able to handle three Korean children who adored your brother and sister-in-law?"

Derry smiled and nodded. "I love them already, and we've forged a strong bond even in this short time we've been together. Could they come in now?"

"Yes. We're almost finished." Wilson went to his office door, opened it, and gestured to the three children sitting stiff-backed on the leather sofa in the waiting room. They came at once and clustered close to Derry, who kissed each in turn.

Wilson's slow smile had a relieved tinge to it as he watched them. "This could be the very help you need to overcome that bottomed out feeling that's the aftermath of divorce."

Derry looked away from him, feeling the tremor in her body and willing herself not to give in to it. "That part of my life is over." She looked at each of the children. "This is my life now . . . all the life I need." The solemn looks of the three pulled at her heart. "We're a family now, aren't we? We'll help each other. Right?"

Three heads nodded in unison, silken hair shimmering.

"See." She looked at Wilson and rose with Baby Sara in her arms, ignoring the frown on the lawyer's face.

"You've lost more weight since I've last seen you, Derry. You're too thin."

"Nonsense. I needed to go on a diet anyway. Derry knew that she was a little on the slim side but her appetite had disappeared after the divorce, then the plane crash that took Dev and Sandy's life seemed to follow right on top of it. Food choked her. For months she had lived on tea and juices it seemed. Now her once muscular figure was honed to greyhound slender. There were hollows under her cheekbones, her peach bloom skin stretched over the skeleton of her face, her sapphire eyes looked enormous, and her neck seemed too fragile to hold the heavy curtain of blue-black hair, which she had twisted into a coil at her nape. Her narrow waist was no more than a handspan now, her hips like a boy's. It irritated her that her bottom seemed no less rounded with the loss of weight, but her legs seemed even longer.

She shifted the little girl higher on her shoulder so that she could shake hands with Wilson. "Thank you for all you've done. And please don't worry about us. We'll be fine. Bring Maddy and come out to Laneport one evening and have dinner with us. Now that the days are getting longer we might even be able to sit outside."

Kimberley and Sara, the five-year-old and three-year-old, took her hand when they left Wilson's office. Lee—who was named for Derry's maternal grandfather, a true Southern gentleman by the name of Carruthers Lee Calhoun—walked alone, as a proud, seven-year-old man must.

Derry smiled to herself as she ushered the children into the car. How ironic that Kim and Lee should have such deceptively-sounding Oriental names—when in fact they were named after two such hidebound Americans as Grandpa Calhoun and their maternal grandmother, Kimberley Durant.

Before starting the car she turned to look at the children. "We still don't know each other too well because you lived so long in Japan, but we are going to be friends. You see, I love you very much; you are all of Dev and Sandy that I have and now you are mine." She felt tears in her eyes when the three of them looked at her with such solemnity and sadness. Derry had made up her mind not to pretend their parents would be coming back, nor to pretend they had never existed. "It will be hard for all of us, but we'll struggle together and not let your Mom and Dad down."

"No, we won't do that." Lee spoke for the girls, who were holding hands and watching Derry. "We'll help you, Derry."

"Thank you."

She made lasagne for dinner that night and was delighted when the children smiled and tucked in the food with a normal appetite. Somehow it made the meal taste better to Derry.

After eating she asked them if they would like to stroll around the large yard. It was the main part of the property that had come to her from her parents, who had died within days of each other two years after she and Aaron had been married. There was a three-acre lawn area around the house; the rest of the acreage was leased to a farmer who raised corn and alfalfa. Despite the rural atmosphere, they were only a short drive outside the town of Laneport, whose chief claim to fame was a section of the State University System of New York called Laneport University. Derry had graduated from the university as had her brother, who had gone on to get an M.S. degree, then a Ph.D. in mathematics. It was while he was a professor at Tokyo University that he and Sandy had adpoted their three children from an orphanage devoted to caring for children of mixed parentage. The little ones came from all over Southeast Asia.

Derry watched Sara, Kim, and Lee play with Milo, an easygoing German shepherd. The dog had taken to them at once. "Actually," Derry told the children, "Milo is supposed to be my watch dog while I'm in the city at my job. I'm afraid, though, that he'd lead a burglar to the silver and wag his tail as if saying 'help yourself.' "

Kim, the five-year-old, giggled, and Lee smiled, but Baby Sara hugged the German shepherd, telling him in her adorable lisp that he was not to worry, she would take care of the burglars.

Derry took a deep breath. "Tomorrow a friend of mine, Gerard Holden, is coming to the house. I think he would make a good father for you and he is anxious to meet you."

"Is he like Da?" Sara asked, her silky black hair lifting in the early evening breeze.

"No one is like Da," Lee informed her.

Derry looked down at them in the gathering dusk, the spring twilight going chill all at once. Then Aaron's face was there. She could picture him smiling at the children. With great concentration she blotted him from her mind—as she'd taught herself to do. "You're right. No one is like Da. I loved my brother, too." She touched Lee and Kim on the head and lifted baby Sara into her arms. "But we'll be happy. We'll help each other." She felt the two walking at either side take hold of a jeans pocket. At that moment she decided that she would marry Gerard Holden. Her eyes stung for a moment as she thought of Aaron. Why? Why, had she thought of him so much today? Sometimes days would go by and she wouldn't think of him, or of their marriage, at all.

She made a big fuss of taking baths, letting Sara and Kim linger in the bubbly water. She skipped over to the other bathroom to check on Lee.

"You'll turn into a prune," she yelled through the door, watching the steam puff from the shower stall.

"I like it," he yelled back.

"You're just like your father. He used to take all the hot water before I would have a chance to shower." Her voice was still raised. It gave her a dart of pleasure when she heard the boy chuckle. "This was his bathroom when he was a boy. And when he became a teenager my father had to install another water heater."

The girls loved their pink and cream bathroom and told Derry that they could clean it up themselves. They proceeded to spray the bathroom tiles with cleanser and wipe them with paper towels. It gave Derry a lump in the throat to watch baby Sara push her tongue out the side of her mouth as she scrubbed the side of the tub.

She held her breath as she finished tucking the children into bed. She prayed there would be no nightmare tonight with Kim crying aloud for Da.

Lee and Sara had been unable to hold back their own tears and often Derry had held them and cried herself.

She waited an hour before calling Gerard, wanting to be sure the children were truly settled before she committed herself to being on the telephone.

"I hope you have decided in my favor, Derry," Gerard stated in his formal way after they'd finished with the niceties.

Just for once it wouldn't have hurt him to act excited about marrying her, Derry thought, then chided herself, remembering that Gerard's calmness was just what she needed to raise children. God forbid that she should try to do so within the hurricanelike atmosphere that prevailed throughout her marriage to Aaron. Remembering the discomfort she had often felt with his fast lane friends made Derry shiver. "I have, Gerard. Perhaps you could come earlier tomorrow and have dinner with all of us."

There was a long silence. "My calendar seems free. Yes I could come to dinner. I think it would be good for the children to meet me as soon as possible. They should know right away that I will be a firm disciplinarian, but—"

"Gerard, the children are my responsibility," Derry pointed out, her voice mild.

"Of course, technically, they are, dear." Gerard was painstakingly fair at all times. "But, since I will be their father, they will have to understand that I will be in charge. You do see the wisdom of that, don't you? You wouldn't want them to be fractious and unmanageable because of a lack of discipline would you?"

"No, but—"

"Ah, I knew you would see it my way!" He wanted to set the date and place for their wedding, he told her. Derry thought he seemed to be in an awful rush, but didn't object. It was only when she put down the phone that she felt the nigglings of apprehension curling in her stomach.

When she hurried from work the next evening, hoping to beat the traffic, she blessed the fates that had induced her to make soup a few days before and freeze it. She would serve the cauliflower soup after a fruitcup of fresh peaches in raspberry sauce. Filet of Sole Fournier with a spinach salad would be easy to prepare quickly and delicious, and brownies with a scoop of ice cream would be just right for dessert. She was congratulating herself on menu planning when she saw the traffic jam ahead on the expressway. The twenty-five miles would take twice as long to drive now. Derry groaned and shifted into low. She would soon have to trade in the two-seater sports car for something bigger and the thought gave her a wrench.

By the time she reached her community she was an hour later than usual. As she pulled into the long driveway, Kim skipped across the lawn to meet her, Milo at her heels. Jenny Lisman, the baby-sitter, came onto the porch carrying Sara. Lee was nowhere in sight.

"Lee was in a fight," Kim carolled; she was getting more American and more talkative by the minute. "He didn't let Timmy Dearborn bully me."

"Is he hurt?" Derry looked up at teenaged Jenny who took over the care of the children from her mother, Linda Lisman, when she got home from the local high school. The girl shook her head as she descended the steps of the porch. She still carried the baby, who held out her chubby arms to Derry.

Derry took the sweet-smelling Sara into her arms and kissed her plump cheek. "And has my baby been good all day?"

"Not baby," Sara said, her olive skin creasing in a smile. "Big girl."

Jenny left, assuring Derry that things were fine and that she would be able to baby-sit on Friday. That was the evening on which Gerard's bank held its annual spring dinner. Derry had agreed to go with him.

Lee came into the house while Derry was stirring the sauce for the Sole Fournier. He stood and looked at her, his hands hanging at his sides, an abrasion on his cheek.

Derry kept stirring, curbing the inclination to leap across the room and sweep him up into her arms. "Your father used to do better than that. He usually came home with a shiner." Derry tasted the sauce, wincing at its heat.

There was a long silence. Derry just kept stirring then, adding a bit more white pepper and a touch more marjoram.

"You should see the other guy," Lee said in accented English.

She whirled around from the stove, biting her lip and blinking at the slow smile spreading across Lee's face. "I didn't notice the cut lip. Do you think you will be able to eat soup and fish?"

Lee nodded. "I like cauliflower soup, and I didn't think I would."

Kim came into the kitchen, leading Sara, their hair shining like liquid coal. "I dressed Sara, and I made gelatin for Lee. Jenny said that it makes you feel good if your lips are sore."

Derry looked at the ladylike child and wondered how she had ever found her life satisfying before Kim and Lee and Sara had entered it. "Thank you for the gelatin, Kim. We'll put it out with the dessert." Derry looked at Lee. "You're right, Kim. It is good for a puffy lip. We'll put it out with the fruit and soup." She smiled at Sara in her ruffled pink dress. "Would you two check the table to see that all is ready?"

When the girls scampered through the swinging door leading to the dining room, she walked over to Lee and put her arms around him. "You're like Dev." As she leaned over him, she felt the two thin arms come up around her waist and his body shudder against hers. She stood there with him like that, swallowing and blinking her eyes until she was sure both of them were composed, then she pushed back from him. "Perhaps you'd like to wear your new blue shirt tonight?"

Lee nodded and left the kitchen.

Gerard arrived promptly at six-thirty. "I really prefer to eat earlier, Derry. I like my long evenings."

"I wasn't even halfway home half an hour ago, Gerard." Derry didn't look at him as she tore the spinach into bite-sized pieces.

The doorbell rang. Gerard looked questioningly at the doorway leading from the kitchen to the oak-panelled hall that spilled into the hexagonal foyer with the stained glass panels in the double front door. "Who could that be, Derry?" he asked.

"I don't know." Derry looked up to say more but stopped as Kim rushed from the hall into the kitchen. "What is it?" Derry asked the child, wiping her hands on a towel, then kneeling in front of the wide-eyed child.

"Timmy Dearborn's father is at the door, and he's calling Lee names." Kim's lip trembled.

Derry rose, feeling an uncomfortable heat rise in her body. She gently moved Kim aside, vaguely aware that Gerard had said something. She could scarcely hear anything because of the roaring in her ears.

A man had his hand on the screen door, which her young handyman had just reinstalled. Derry looked from that hand to his other and felt her anger blaze. The man had taken hold of Lee by the shoulder and was leaning over him, shouting.

"What the bloody hell are you doing to my son?" Derry said, the red mist in front of her eyes making it difficult to distinguish the man's features. "Take your hand away or I'll break your arm."

"Derry!" Lee and Gerard said at the same time, but of course Gerard's voice had more force.

She ignored both of them as she pushed against the man's chest with the flat of her hand. "Don't you *ever* touch him like that again." She felt as though her insides were breaking apart. She always took great pride in controlling her temper, not in displaying it. But for the very first time in her life, she was in the grip of a fury she had not the slightest wish to control. "Get off my porch."

"Now, listen, you. No Chink kid is gonna push my kid around. See?"

"I know the whole story." Derry stepped in front of Lee, shaking off Gerard's arm. "Your son Timmy started it. As far as I'm concerned it is over. If you don't think so, then you start with me, but don't you dare touch my son."

"Stanley Dearborn does business with Laneport Trust," Gerard hissed. "Calm yourself!"

"I don't give a cotton damn," Derry said, letting the screen slam behind her as she stepped further onto the porch. "Mr. Dearborn, you just tell that little bully of yours to stop picking on our Kim! That's what started all this!"

Stanley Dearborn seemed to swell, his squat, muscular body taking on a bulldog stance. "Now you listen to me, sister . . ."

"She's not your sister!" came a firm, imperious voice. Derry couldn't have failed to recognize it. She gasped. When had Aaron driven up the circular driveway? He slammed the door of the Ferrari and stretched to full height. Then, as his long strides carried him across the lawn and over the wide border of late tulips and daffodils that bordered the drive, his hard-packed body seemed to flex itself in readiness. At six-feet-three Aaron Lathrop looked more like one of his construction workers than the director of his worldwide company specializing in designing and building offices, college complexes, condominiums, and apartments. His dark blond hair was sun streaked and had a few silver threads at the temples. The muscular neck and shoulders strained against the linen shirt of deep green that matched the linen slacks hugging his long muscular legs.

Derry swallowed, angry at her quick awareness of how the green of his clothes enhanced the sea green of his eyes. She wondered where he had been to have so deepened the tan of the skin stretched taut over rock hard cheekbones and firm chin. Despite his fine clothes he didn't look Back Bay, Boston. He looked Waterfront, New York. Why was he here now, after all this time? Six months, one week, and . . . Derry cursed herself, clenching the hands at her sides so tightly she could feel the half-moon indentations of fingernails in her palms.

Stanley turned, his stance wary. "Who the hell is this? 'Cause if you are this kid's old man, I think you should talk to your wife *and* your kid. I don't want anybody pushing—"

"And I don't want you coming to this house again intimidating my wife . . . What kid?" Aaron's head slewed around toward Derry, his eyes narrowing on her. "What the hell is he talking about?" Aaron spat the words at her as if they were bullets.

Stanley Dearborn was quiet all at once. So was Gerard, and Lee stopped repeating, "Don't you shout at Derry."

Aaron moved forward like a battering ram. "Tell me."

Derry took one step back, keeping Lee behind her. "I'll tell you nothing." She gulped, then forced herself to look at Stanley Dearborn. "I will tell *you* something, though, and for the last time: Stay away from my child! If you have a complaint, then come to me!"

Stanley, keeping a wary eye on the big guy with the murderous look on his face, began to speak. "Now listen—"

"Get out of here," Aaron snarled.

Stanley muttered, but left hastily.

Derry took a deep breath in order to tell Aaron that he was welcome to drop himself over Niagara Falls with his Ferrari wrapped around his neck. Kim came to the door before she could say a word.

"Derry, I keep stirring but it's getting thick."

"My God, the sauce," Derry screeched. She clutched Kim. "You're such a good girl, but please be careful when you're near the stove, love. You could have been burned." She swept Sara into her arms as she galloped into the kitchen. She set the baby down and looked at the browning lumpy stuff that was to have been her sauce for the Sole Fournier. "Damn you, Stanley Dearborn," she mumbled as she lifted the pan to the sink and heaved the mess into the disposal.

She turned to explain to a pained-looking Gerard and saw Aaron behind him talking to Lee, nodding his head. Kim looked up at him, the back of her head almost parallel to the floor.

When Sara toddled over to him, he leaned over and grinned at the child.

Derry felt such a sharp pain that she thought for a second something in her had torn. Aaron had wanted children. So had she. But she had been unable to conceive. That was one of the reasons she believed they had become estranged.

"Really, dear, couldn't you just make sandwiches for the children and send them to bed? Then we'll have something," Gerard said.

Aaron rose to his feet, looking at the array of food on the counter top: the assorted vegetables, the fish. "Ummm, Sole Fournier. I love it. How would it be if I took the kids outside and reintroduced myself to Milo? Could you make the sauce then?"

"Really!" Gerard glared at Aaron. "Who are you?"

Aaron didn't seem to hear the question as he shepherded the children through the old-fashioned butler's pantry to the back door, a giggling Sara raised to his shoulder.

Derry turned back to her sauce, assembling the ingredients blindly, answering Gerard's questions about Aaron in monosyllables. Why was Aaron here? What made him come tonight of all nights when she wanted the children to get to meet Gerard?

"Derry? Derry, are you listening to me?"

"Huh? What? Oh yes, we'll talk later, Gerard. Take the spinach salads to the table, will you, please?"

"Is that man eating with us?" Gerard put the salads on the tray in perfectly aligned rows.

"Huh? Oh Lord, I don't think so." Derry urged him toward the dining room.

When the door swung shut at his back, she sprinted through the pantry, out the door, and onto the small back porch.

Aaron was pushing Sara on the little swing and Lee was pushing Kim on the bigger one. They were all laughing.

"Dinner!" Derry called. She was rehearsing the words she would say to Aaron, discarding most possibilities, as the children obligingly stopped swinging and Aaron helped Sara down. Then Kim took his hand.

"Don't worry that you won't have enough to feed Aaron," she said. "I told him that I would share my dinner with him."

Sara was hoisted back to her lofty perch on Aaron's wide shoulder. She nodded as her chubby fingers entwined in his sun streaked blond hair. "Me, too," she cooed.

"Aaron says we look like you, Derry, 'cept our eyes are brown." Kim chuckled, her loose front tooth wobbling. "He says you used to wear your hair on your shoulders just like me."

"Me, too," Sara piped again. "I like your boo eyes."

"Thank you, darling." Derry reached up for her. "You must be starving. I have your fish ready for you." She ignored Aaron.

"Good." Sara gave her a sticky kiss on the cheek.

Washing the children would have taken more time if Aaron hadn't taken charge of Sara and Kim. Lee readied himself, of course. By the time they arrived at the table, Gerard was seated at the head and Derry was just placing the steaming soup tureen on the sideboard next to a basket of cloth-covered hot rolls.

"I really prefer to eat my salad before I have my meal, not with it. And of course, gelatin is for dessert," Gerard opined staring at the cauliflower soup.

Derry was going to explain that she put out the food that way for the children's benefit, but when she saw Aaron's amused smile as he held her chair for her, she ground her teeth together and said nothing. She knew that he took the seat next to her because he wanted to irritate her. She had to press her lips together to keep from poking out her tongue at him.

Even Gerard seemed to like the soup and peaches, but he frowned when, during the main course, Lee ate the black raspberry gelatin. "You should eat your spinach, young man. Here, let me put some dressing on it for you."

"No, thank you, sir, I'll eat it plain. The vinegar would sting my mouth." Lee put his hand over his salad as Gerard was about to pour from a cruet.

"I see." Gerard set the cruet down exactly on the spot it had occupied before he lifted it. He shook out his napkin again, dabbed at his mouth, then steepled his hands and cleared his throat. "About the fight, young man—"

"I've all ready spoken to the boy," Aaron said, attacking the sole with his usual gusto.

"I beg your pardon." Gerard glared at Aaron, affronted. "Since I will be the boy's legal guardian in a month or so, I must tell you that I don't like your interference and—"

"What are you saying?" Aaron snarled, making every head swivel toward him.

Derry took a deep breath. "If you would listen when I speak to you instead of writing off every word I say—" Derry snapped. She pressed her lips together and took a calming breath. "I think I told you that Sandy and Dev were killed." She looked at the children, smiling at each one in turn.

"I got your message when I returned from Senegal," Aaron said in a strained tone. "I got back late last night. My office couldn't have reached me to forward the message." His graven face was softened. "I wanted to tell you how sorry I was. I was very fond of both of them." His glance slid over the children. He, too, smiled at each in turn. "I

knew about the kids of course, but I didn't realize
that you would have sole custody of them."

"Until our marriage next month, of course." Gerard dabbed at his mouth with the napkin and
pushed his plate to one side. "Then, as their father, I shall be taking over the charge of the
children."

"Oh?" Aaron leaned back in his chair. "I didn't
know you had planned to marry so soon, Derry."
The Back Bay accent seemed more pronounced,
making Derry wince. Aaron was losing his temper.

She cleared her throat. "Gerard and I decided to
marry to give the children the stability of family
life."

"You never thought to mention this to me?"
The bland tone would have been a clue only to
those closest to Aaron.

Derry geared herself for battle. "Now see here,
Aaron—"

"Now, now, dear, no need to raise your voice."
Gerard leaned sideways so that he could see around
the Lenox bowl of daffodils and baby's breath. He
smiled. "Lathrop seems to understand."

"Does he?" Derry muttered, her eyes fixing on
Aaron's sea green eyes, then sliding away. "Don't
bet on it," she muttered to the last morsel of sole
she was pushing around on her plate.

Aaron rose to his feet. "Shall I get the dessert?
The coffee?"

"Don't bother," Derry snarled, rising quickly and
stacking plates with unnecessary force. She fumed
when Aaron directed the children to help her and
they jumped to do it. She would have asked them
herself. "Damn and blast that man. Why doesn't
he get lost?" she muttered to the stacked plates.

She had her head down and rammed the swinging door. She turned on the water in the sink to

soak the pans and rinse the dishes she would be putting in the dishwasher.

Aaron popped into the kitchen. "You're really going to marry that pompous ass?" The words fired from his mouth like missiles, but the hand he placed on her behind as she bent over the dishwasher was gentle, petting, familiar.

"Stop that." She straightened and turned to face him. "It is none of your business what I do with my life, just as it is none of my business what you do."

"Stop talking like your pompous friend." Aaron's body was a menacing curve as he looked down at her.

"Don't call him pompous," Derry shot back.

Aaron ignored her words. "And on what date are you marrying him?"

"Not that it is any of your business, but I am marrying Gerard on the twenty-first. Reverend Talbot is marrying us in the University Interfaith Chapel, and the children are to be my attendants."

"A little different from our marriage at St. Luke's, isn't it?"

"If you mean that Beacon Hill society won't be in attendance, then you're right." Once she began she couldn't seem to stop. "If you mean that your mother and Aunt Sylvie won't pick apart the reception, my family and friends, then you're right. If you mean that you won't be off in a corner, planning some get together with your fast lane cronies, then you're right again."

"I never did that on our wedding day. I never left your side. I never wanted to." Aaron hissed the words.

"Really? How quickly you got over such foolishness. A month after we married, you left for Manila." Derry exhaled sharply.

"That was business," Aaron barked.

"Del Peters took his wife, Grant Richards took his live-in." Derry sliced open old wounds.

"Derry, for God's sake, I explained . . ." Aaron pushed one large well-shaped hand through his combed back hair, the disordered wave falling forward at once.

Derry held up one hand, palm outward. "You're right. It's years old news. We won't discuss it." The palm closed into a fist. "Just remember that I'm marrying Gerard and that it has nothing to do with you."

"Oh, you think so, do you?" The clipped Harvard accent was iron hard. Aaron spun on his heel and stormed out of the kitchen, leaving Derry breathless and angry.

It was a shock when the dream came again. It had been days since it had invaded her unconscious. She knew with a helpless sense of dismay that it was useless to try and fight it. The dream always won.

She groaned as she replayed the scene in which she, a starry eyed eighteen-year-old accepted a flawless marquise diamond from the man who was eleven years her senior. Even her unsophisticated eyes could tell it was a multi-carat stone, fabulously expensive. She gasped with pain as she saw the glowing bride. Her black hair was like a cape under an exquisite, cathedral-length train in handwrought Majorcan lace. It had belonged to Aaron's grandmother.

"You are an alien in St. Luke's cathedral just as you are in the Lathrop family," she muttered in warning to the bride who ignored her voice. "They will let you know fast enough that you don't belong." Derry tried to scream to the dewy-eyed girl in white but no sound came.

"I love you," Aaron had whispered when they were finally alone. He said it over and over to her, too, in the bedroom of the pink stucco home called Windrift in Bermuda when he'd begun to minister to her in the slow, volcanic way that had her writhing under him.

She had been surprised and thrilled when he had kissed all of her body, invading her with hands, mouth and at the last his body. "I love you." Derry whispered.

She awoke suddenly, sweat dripping down her face. She sobbed into her pillow.

"I'll marry Gerard. I will. The children will be happy. We *will* be happy." She punched her pillow between sobs.

Three

Derry couldn't believe this was her wedding day. The past month had flown.

She looked at the three pairs of eyes, seal brown and soft, staring at her in the mirror, and felt her own eyes mist with tears. She smiled. They were worth anything. She tamped down the doubts she had about marrying Gerard, and made a vow that these children would be happy. Aaron would not have been as solid an influence as Gerard. Aaron! Damn! What made her think of him now? She had spent the better part of this month jamming him out of her mind. It had set her teeth on edge when Sara and Kim had kept asking about him. Lee had said nothing, but he had watched her with eyes that seemed to see through her skin.

She sighed and studied her mirror image, liking the teal blue silk even more now than when she had purchased it. The color enhanced the turquoise of her eyes and seemed to add blue lights to her ebony hair, which hung like a black drape to her shoulders. The Grecian-style dress just touched the tops of her shoes, the figure-hugging silk defining her firm, high breasts, narrow waist and hips, and long legs. At five-feet-eight in bare feet, she was only two inches shorter than her groom. Today she wore low heels, not the high heels she was addicted to and which flattered her trim legs.

She took a deep breath, turned to face the children, then nodded that she was ready.

The ride to the University Interfaith Chapel took mere minutes. Derry's own property abutted the campus, and they could have walked diagonally across the farm property and been there at almost the same time it took them to drive around its perimeter.

"I'm very proud of you today," Derry whispered to the children. The Cadillac—driven by George Lisman, whose father, George, Sr., was giving Derry away—pulled up and parked in front of the chapel. George was allowed to drive this car only on special occasions.

"Kim, you and Sara look like pink angels in your dresses and . . ." She looked at Lee sitting on the jump seat in his blue suit. "You look like the man of the house."

There was a flurry of greetings as they alighted from the car, and Derry and the children took the time to speak to everyone.

"Derry, my dear, you look thinner than the first time you married. Doesn't she Ira?" Theo Halley screeched to her husband. He nodded as usual. "She's gotta family now. That'll fatten her up." Theo's voice went up a decibel. Her husband nodded. Animals sensitive to noise scattered. Other neighbors tittered. Kim stared at her open-mouthed. Sara's lower lip trembled.

Then they were inside the chapel, listening to

the murmurs of the small number of people all ready seated for the wedding. It would not be a large gathering. Derry had wanted it small. Gerard had wanted it inexpensive.

"Derry, you look lovely." Linda Lisman said, clutching her attendant's bouquet. "I don't know why I'm so nervous. You're the bride." Linda cast an appraising eye over the children, a proud look on her face. "They do look wonderful, don't they?"

"Yes." Derry released Sara to Lee's keeping and freed Kim's hand so that she could take the flowers Linda handed to her.

The organ played a crescendo and Linda looked at her wildly and took her place on the aisle. When Derry looked around for the children, they'd vanished. "Linda, did Jenny take the children?" Her words died in her throat. Aaron was coming through the church vestibule, directly toward her. His face looked as though it had been hewn from rock; his eyes held the fire of fanatical purpose.

"What are you . . . Hey! Stop that," Derry gasped as Aaron swept her off her feet. "Stop," she cried as he started toward the door. She pummelled his chest as he ran down the steps with her in his arms, openmouthed people standing back to let them pass. She saw George shout something and point, but she couldn't hear because of the roaring in her ears.

Aaron dumped her into the passenger seat of the Ferrari. She stared, flabberghasted, at the three children sitting in the narrow area behind the front seats. They grinned at Derry and said "Hi" in unison.

The car roared away from the curb almost giving Derry whiplash.

Lee said, "This is great. How fast will it go?"

Kim said, "I like Aaron."

Sara said, "Me, too."

Derry yelped. Glancing back at the gleeful children, then at Aaron, she said, "Take me back at once." She wanted to punch him in the nose. "This is kidnapping." Her voice was rising despite her efforts. "Where are you taking me?"

"To get married," Aaron answered, slewing the low-slung car around a corner without lessening speed. The car climbed a ramp and, with another thrust of power, shot onto the thruway.

"Never!" Derry inhaled. "Do you think I'm a masochist? Do you think I'd trade my peace of mind for another ride on that rollercoaster you call life?"

"I've changed." Aaron geared down and swung around a slower vehicle.

"Bull!" Derry bit her lip and glanced at the children again. How could they look so unconcerned while they were being kidnapped? "You'd never change. I will *not* marry you."

"You'll either marry me, or we'll just live together." Aaron spoke through a jaw that seemed filled with stones. "You are not marrying that pluperfect ass, Derry, so forget it." The car roared off the thruway and down a lesser highway. "I'm through indulging you. You're a grown woman. It's time you accepted your responsibilities to me and to yourself."

"What in blue blazes are you talking about?" Derry's head swivelled to take in the passing scenery. "Are we heading toward the airport?" She could hear the hoarseness in her own voice.

"Right."

"I'll have you arrested. I'll call the FBI." She gasped.

"Damn you, Derry, you are not going to marry that fool! You need a father for those children and it's going to be me. So sit back and enjoy the ride."

Derry could feel herself balloon with anger. She

called to mind a dozen epithets and hurled them at him silently. She could feel the enamel being ground off her teeth. "Have you forgotten why we divorced?"

"I never *knew* why we divorced. I never wanted the divorce," Aaron answered. He had no pity for the Ferrari—or their spines—as he roared along a bumpy side street.

Derry tried to keep her voice from quavering as they sailed down the rutted street. "You know damn well why!" she hissed. "You were never home. Everything was business in the day, business dinners at night, no rest, no relaxation, not talking to one another . . ."

"I kept you with me as much as possible," Aaron snarled, a dark red creeping up his neck.

"Always in a crowd, never able to say more than a few words to each other, then home again to drop into bed exhausted and sleep until the merry go round started the next day."

"I can remember many times that we didn't sleep . . . that we made love all night . . ." Aaron stated, his tones slurring.

"Stop it." Derry looked back at the goggle-eyed children. She handed her bouquet of stephanotis with one orchid to the girls, suddenly not wanting to look at it. Suddenly relieved to be with Aaron . . . not stuffy Gerard.

Aaron screeched around another corner and zoomed through opened gates leading onto the Page Airways property.

"You don't keep a plane here anymore," Derry protested, hoping she was right.

"How the hell do you know what I do?" Aaron had an irritated look on his face as he pulled her from the car and directed the children out of the back.

Sara was only too glad to be lifted onto Aaron's

shoulders and chortled with glee at being so high. She patted Aaron's cheek with one chubby hand.

Derry glared up at the traitorous Sara who grinned back toothily. She tried to pry free of the hand with which Aaron imprisoned her arm. "You cannot kidnap us." She could hear the bluster in her voice. For long seconds she toyed with the idea of shouting for help to the mechanics working in the hangars, but the thought of how upset the children would become by such a brouhaha stilled her.

She stared at the Lear Jet already warming up, the cigar chewing man standing at the top of the short rise of stairs familiar to her. "Barrow . . . you . . . here . . ."

"Howdy, Mrs. Lathrop. Welcome aboard 'The Derry.' " He reached down to assist her up the last step into the plane, his bland smile ignoring her expression of outrage. "You look mighty pretty. Just right for a wedding. Should reach the chapel in time." He turned away from her and walked into the cockpit.

Derry heard the clanging sound of the door shutting, mouth agape as she watched Aaron strap the children into their seats, then gesture for her to be seated as well. She allowed him to snap her seatbelt before she thought to struggle. "You— you brigand . . . pirate . . . hijacker," she stuttered in hissing tones. "You can't do this."

The children stared at her in complacent interest.

"Are those dirty words, Derry?" Kim asked, placing Sara's blanket into the baby's arms.

Derry stared at the child. "No, of course not, dear." She tried to smile but her face had a rubbery quality to it and wouldn't respond.

"Are you going to marry Aaron now? Will he be our new daddy?" Kim stared at her.

Baby Sara looked at Derry. "Love Aaron."

Lee stared at her, a shutter dropping over his eyes.

Derry stared around the interior of the plane, taking numb inventory of the real leather on the seats, the hardwood table screwed on the floor. Aaron had gone through into the cockpit to be copilot, she assumed, as he always had when not doing the flying himself. She looked back at the children and inhaled deeply. "You don't mind that we are flying away from Gerard? That he won't be your father now?"

Lee cleared his throat. "We want you to be happy, Derry."

"But you like Aaron?" she asked, a prickling horror filling her as she waited for the answer.

They nodded as one.

"I see."

The children fell asleep one by one, Lee giving her a smile even as his lids fluttered closed.

Derry sat there, fingers hurting as she wrung them together. How could she bear being married to Aaron again? Yet she couldn't just live with him. Oh, God, what must Gerard be thinking? She knew a sudden stab of guilt. She didn't really *care* what Gerard was thinking. How horrible! How could she have been about to go through with the marriage to him? She closed her eyes. She had *wanted* Aaron to save her from herself and her stupid notions of stability. Unconsciously, she'd yearned for Aaron to reclaim her. She sighed and looked out the window at the creamy clouds scudding beneath them. Her eyes felt too heavy at the moment.

Derry had no idea why she was in the rowboat in the middle of the ocean during a terrible storm. The boat rocked furiously.

"Come on, Derry, wake up. We're landing."

"Huh?" Aaron had been the rowboat in the ocean that she dreamed about. It was he shaking her awake. "Where are we?"

"Maryland. We're to be married in less than an hour, unless you would prefer the alternative?"

Derry glowered at him, trying to wipe the sleep from her eyes. "We'll be married," she hissed at him, keeping a wary eye on Kim and Lee in case they were listening. "But it's a fiasco, a—a cup of water from a poisoned well. It didn't work before. It won't—"

"I'd love to chat with you," Aaron interrupted her. "But we're on a tight schedule."

"It won't work," Derry gritted out, as Aaron half carried her from the plane.

Barrow had a car waiting, motor running, and he stayed behind the wheel as Aaron shepherded the others into the back.

Derry had only been to Maryland once before when Aaron had flown them to a restaurant on Chesapeake Bay that specialized in Maryland crab. Now she looked at the passing scenery with glazed eyes. I am going to remarry Aaron, she thought, the phrase repeating and repeating in her mind as the car sped to it's destination. Oh God! She bit her lip. I'm not miserable about it. I don't hate it. Oh, damn my insides! I love him. I hate myself for loving him. Why did he have to come back into my life?

"Gas pains, love?" Aaron leaned over and covered the hand clenching and unclenching on her abdomen. "I'll get you some soda water."

"*You're* my gas pains," Derry shot back.

"I remember how sensitive your tummy was when we travelled," Aaron mused, his eyes having a faraway look. "I always had to make sure that you stayed regular."

"You did not." Derry reddened, her eyes flicking toward the children. "My—my stomach has nothing to do with you."

"Ah, here we are." They pulled to a stop and Aaron whisked them out of the car.

Derry had a hazy perception of a fieldstone building with stained glass windows, then she was walking down a short aisle, the children around her and Aaron, and Barrow bringing up the rear.

"What? No Ern Griswold as best man?" Derry asked dazedly.

"No," Aaron snarled, startling her.

She couldn't have said what the vows consisted of, but she heard herself mumble, "I will." She tried to smile at the young clergyman in the gray suit when she realized that he had just given her his best wishes but her lips were cardboard stiff.

The time it took to return to the plane seemed shorter, but Derry was sure that was because she couldn't seem to climb out of the daze she had been in since the beginning of the ceremony.

"I like to fly." Kim smiled at Aaron, letting him tighten her safety belt.

"Ears hurt." Sara's lips trembled, as the plane climbed.

Aaron stayed in the cabin with them and when the baby said this he loosened her belt and swept her into his arms whispering to her.

Derry watched the baby hold tightly to Aaron's neck, and she wished that it were her arms that were there. She gasped and clutched her stomach at the thought.

"Tummy again, love?"

"No," she snapped, glaring at him. "Where are we going? I must call Gerard."

"To the apartment in New York. Tomorrow we'll finish the rest of our trip." Aaron's eyes radiated over her.

"And then we are going to St. Thomas where your latest construction project is taking shape?" Derry watched him as a mongoose watches a cobra.

"I *did* mention that we are doing work in St. Thomas." Aaron let the baby slide down his chest so that she was cradled more comfortably. He continued to murmur words to her until her head was nodding.

"I intend to inform Gerard where I am." Derry held herself stiffly against Aaron's gaze, for every time he looked at her now, a spasm of reaction rocked her body.

This time when Aaron looked at her, his eyes were like glittering emeralds. "I prefer that my wife not call other men."

"*Your wife?*" Derry sputtered, then remembered. "Ah . . . well this marriage could hardly count as *real.*" She swallowed hard under Aaron's fierce green stare. "Why are we stopping in New York?"

"To give the children a rest and to introduce them to their nanny." Aaron rose and placed Sara on a seat, pulling at the bottom of the seat until metal slats rose at the side. There was even a bumper to place next to the slats so that Sara was cocooned in safety; it was much the same as being in a crib.

"Nanny?" Derry's voice was squeaky. "These are my children. I'll take care of them."

"Correction. These are *our* children now, and you need a break now and then." Aaron held up his hand. "Don't argue, Derry. You won't be losing any of your rights as a mother. You just won't be run ragged." He sat down next to her, reaching across to lift her left hand to his mouth, touching his lips to her rings. "Are you happy to have your rings back where they belong?"

"I'm surprised that you kept them." Derry tried to clear the hoarseness from her throat, her eyes going to Kim and Lee who were playing dominoes at the table.

"I've kept all your things." Aaron's voice was a harsh purr. "All those things you told me you didn't want, that I had given you, that you threw back in my face."

"I didn't!" Derry could feel the old core of anger heating up. "Nothing you gave me belonged to me." The pressure on her hand increased until she thought her bones would be reduced to jelly.

"What the hell do you mean? Everything I gave you was in your name, to do with as you wished." His body partially screened the children from her sight.

"Really? Is that why I heard from all the Lathrops about my duty to care for things belonging to the family for generations? Is that why I was constantly reminded of my role as caretaker, not owner. Lord, it was like being married to the Smithsonian."

"Damn it, Derry, I told you a hundred times to ignore my family. What I gave you was mine to give and yours to do with as you wished. They still are and you're getting all of them back. Try being an adult about those possessions." He threw her hand back into her lap, fury emanating from him in waves. "*You* own them. *You* can bloody well throw the whole lot away. I'll buy *you* new things and *you* can throw those away too."

"Oh you're a—a—an insensitive—"

"Not insensitive, Derry, my love. Maybe after the job you did on me, I'm a little *de*sensitized, but never insensitive. You should have seen me in the months after you left me. You would have loved it. I was wide open, raw and bleeding to death." He bared his teeth. "I'll never let you do that to me again."

"I had heard you were drinking. I hated hearing

that, but . . ." Derry faltered, remembering how appalled she had been when a friend had described Aaron's condition at a party.

"Drinking? Don't sugar coat it. I was drunk twenty-four hours a day. I got up drunk and went to bed the same way. You almost finished me, devil doll. Never again."

"Aaron." Derry felt her insides begin to shred. "I didn't . . . I didn't want that. I never wanted you to be unhappy."

"No? Yet you left me without a backward glance. You never answered my calls. You hung up on me when I did reach you. You wouldn't meet with me. You wanted to hurt me all right, you wanted me unhappy."

"Whether you believe it or not, I did not leave you to hurt you." How could she tell him that she left because she couldn't bear for him to leave her? She had hung on for nine years because she'd kept hoping that the pressures of his family's dislike, his long working days, his sophisticated, fast lane friends would let up. But the pressures didn't relent, they mounted. How could she tell him that if she had answered even one of his calls in the early days after leaving him, the sound of his voice would have had her crawling back to him?

"I don't know what you're plotting now, wife of mine, but forget any plans you may have of writing off this marriage. This is for real *and* forever." He snarled this then rose to his feet. "We'll be landing in New York in a few minutes. I'm going to help Barrow bring her in to La Guardia."

Derry sat there, shaking, her mind numb.

When the "No Smoking" light came on she fastened the children's safety belts and checked the sleeping Sara in her criblike seat.

La Guardia was a beehive as usual. Derry was

grateful for the efficient way Aaron got them to the car he had arranged to have meet them.

The children oohed and aahed over the limousine, but Derry sat back against the gray velour upholstery with a sigh. She was silent during the half hour ride to the East Seventies in Manhattan.

On their arrival at the apartment house, the doorman came forward at once. "It's nice to see you back, Mrs. Lathrop."

"Thank you, Mills. It's good to see you again, too."

When the elevator doors opened into the foyer a wave of memories rose like a suffocating cloud around Derry. She scarcely noticed the pristine, fortyish woman standing near the wall.

"Good evening, madam. I'm Telford, the children's nanny."

"What? Oh yes." Derry put out her hand, her eyes taking note of the woman's smile, which touched her for a moment then fixed on the children.

"I'll take them, Mrs. Lathrop. I have their dinner all ready and then I'm sure they would like a wash." Telford cocked her head at the staring Lee, the smile turning into a grin. "Of course I realize that a gentleman of your age needs no help, but I thought you might like to give me a hand with the girls."

Lee stared for long moments, then nodded once, taking hold of Kim's hand as Telford lifted a wide-eyed Sara into her arms.

Derry stood there watching the swinging door through which they'd gone, until she felt a hand at the base of her spine.

"Don't worry, darling. Telford is good. Her references are unimpeachable; they were thoroughly checked." Aaron led her up the stairway, whose oaken planks seemed to float on a wrought iron frame.

"Yes, I'm sure you had the well-trained Lathrop army check her back to her kindergarten days."

"Back to her christening, actually." Aaron laughed at the fuming look she gave him. "I took the liberty of hijacking a lot of children's clothing, too. More of the Lathrop army's work. You'll find their suitcases are here, and well filled.

"I should have known," Derry muttered. "I'd like to freshen up. I can use the guest wing."

"You'll use our room. There are two bathrooms in our suite—or have you forgotten?"

Derry looked away from him and around the beige and cream bedroom accented with turquoise, which she herself had decorated. The pain was so sharp she had to bite her lip to keep a moan from escaping. God, how happy she had been in this room . . . at first. Aaron had been so loving, so gentle when they had spent their wedding night here. "Would you mind leaving so that I can change?"

"This time I'll go. But not again, devil doll. You're my wife—the way you've always been my wife—and we are going to be together." The violent slam of the door made a figurine topple from its niche in the wall.

Derry blinked for long moments at the shards of Ainsley that lay on the fluffy champagne-colored wall to wall carpet. She stepped over the pieces of porcelain and went to the phone to dial Gerard's number. He answered on the fifth ring, his voice raised over the background noise of other voices.

"Gerard? Yes, it's me, Derry . . . No, I didn't want to come with him!" She paused and took a deep breath. "We'll be going to St. Thomas, I think. No, I can't leave now. I'm—I'm married. Gerard, I am sorry. Truly. . . . Gerard? Gerard?" Derry looked at the phone in her hand, realizing that the connection was broken. Well, that was that! She *must* have been out of her mind to think she could have made a happy home life for the children with that stuffed shirt!

The shower refreshed her and she stayed under it for a long time, letting the needle spray as hard as pumice onto her body. She shampooed her hair as well, even though she had shampooed it that morning. With her head wrapped in a towel, she smoothed moisturizer on her face, then prepared for bed. As hungry as she was, she was not going downstairs to eat with Aaron. She would just starve until morning. She combed her hair under the red light in the ceiling of the bathroom until it was dry enough to brush. The vigorous strokes she gave it made the heavy, dark mane shine as it became silky soft.

She slipped on a silk wrap she had purchased for her honeymoon with Gerard, then opened the door to the bedroom. She let out a startled gasp. Aaron was arranging dishes on the small table in the bedroom alcove. He removed a steaming platter from the hot cart he'd obviously brought up in the small elevator that went from the kitchen to the second floor hall. He wore a terry cloth wraparound that only reached to mid thigh and left his torso bare.

"Hello, Darling," Aaron called as if he'd known the second she'd emerged from the bathroom. He turned and held out his hands in invitation. "Come and sit down. I have our supper here, our wedding supper." He handed her a tulip-shaped glass frothing with champagne. "Let's drink to our future together."

"No." Derry looked at the precious crystal as though it held acid. "What are you doing here?"

"What any man would be doing on his wedding night. I'm going to feed you and wine you. Then I'm going to take you to bed and make love to you."

"The devil you will!"

"Whether I'm devil or angel, I'm taking you tonight! Not just because I want you—and I do want you, Derry—but because you want me, too." Aaron covered the distance between them. "And don't bother to deny it. Your body is shaking from head to toe like an aspen in a high wind." He plunked down the expensive crystal goblet on the bedside table. Champagne splashed over the side and spilled onto the highly polished rosewood.

Four

Derry felt paralyzed as Aaron stalked around the bed toward her. Every hair on her body rose as though a charge emanating from him touched her. "Food." The squeaky gasp was all she could manage as she felt herself pulled against that muscular body.

Aaron stared down at her, one hand stroking back the hair from her face. "Your hair is like blue-black velvet. I'd dream about it draped over my face as you lay on top of me. Do you remember how we would go to our private beach and—"

"I don't want to talk about Bermuda. That's in the past. I don't think of it any more." She tried to wriggle free with arms gone boneless as the hot memories of the semitropical island washed through her mind.

"Don't you?" Aaron lifted her straight up his body until their faces were touching evenly. "I remember it all." His tongue licked down her cheek.

"Did I ever tell you that my ancestors on my mother's side were pirates based in Bermuda?"

"I knew there had to be brigands there somewhere. The skull and crossbones seem an integral part of your family. Your Aunt Sylvie is a prime example of pure poison." Derry's lips feathered his cheek.

"I always told you to ignore Aunt Sylvie. Her bark is worse than her bite."

"Said the wolf to the lamb." Derry's fingers were tugging at the hair at his nape, the feel of that crispness an erotic stimulus. "Food's getting cold."

"Yes." Aaron's eyes had an opalescent gleam, his words were slurred, and his hands opened and closed on her body in gentle possessiveness.

Blood pounded in Derry's ears, blotting out the thoughts of reason that advised to break free of him. I'm his wife, she told herself, her body quivering in glad despair. She lifted her mouth, taking tiny bites of his chin, relaxing against him, loving the feel of him against her. She felt one broad palm come up and ease the silken wrap from her shoulder. She shrugged, back on that side so his hand could slide down to fondle and cup the swelling fullness of her breast. He lifted her and his mouth took the place of his hand, the pulling and sucking sensation sending rivers of feeling down her body.

"Damn you, Derry, for leaving me." Aaron's guttural whisper was the only sound as he swept her high into his arms and strode toward the bed. His body followed hers downward as though they were one, the taut thighs pressing into her, his open-mouthed aggression coursing over her body. "You'll never leave me again."

Derry wasn't even sure if she heard him right as her own body seemed to flow like molten lava into his, her limbs reaching out for his as though for life. It gave her a perverse feeling of justice when she felt his muscles tremble under her touch. Her nails scraped down his back. Inflamed by Aaron's continuous stroking, Derry's abdomen contracted, her skin sending out a signal of tingling need. She could not deny this man or her need of him. "Children." The hoarseness of her voice surprised her.

"Fine, my lovely devil doll. Just fine." Aaron let his mouth travel in slow quest down her body: her navel, her hipbone, her inner thigh, her knee, her instep, her ankle, the sole of her foot were all ministered to with loving concentration. He fixed her trembling limbs to the bed with the lightest touch of his mouth.

Derry was in the grip of a helpless joy, a bottomless longing that she realized had never gone from her. For long moments she stared into the hectic flush of his face after his return up her form. The heat from his eyes ignited her even more and she heard her own moan as she reached up to clasp his face between her hands. "Aaron. . . . Aaron."

"My God, Derry, it's been so long . . . so long."

She could feel his body surge into hers and she came alive wildly in his arms, feeling her own body push upward in union with his. She was unaware of her nails digging into him as she strove to hold him even closer, to imprison him in her body. For these few moments he was totally hers as she was totally his.

She felt taken with the driving motion, lifted into a kaleidoscopic world where fiercely bright sensations colored every rapturous second. She cried out as the final brilliant explosion tore through her body. Aaron's hoarse, long drawn out groan of fulfillment gave her a deeply tender thrill. They descended together in sweet peace, Aaron holding her, murmuring to her, kissing her gently.

"Hungry." Derry yawned, her jaw cracking as Aaron chuckled into her ear.

"How the hell did you get so skinny with an appetite like yours?" He lifted her up to stand next to the bed before wrapping the silk robe around her. He had paused before tying it at her waist, staring at her nude form. "You're lovely."

She gulped when she heard the deepened tone of his voice. "Do you think the food is spoiled?" She tried to keep her equilibrium while Aaron's eyes roved over her.

"Uhhh? What?" Aaron had to force himself to look at the food, it seemed to Derry, then he frowned at it. "If it is, I'll get more."

She moved back from him and then around him toward the steam table. To her surprise the food was still hot. The salad looked limp, but there was plenty of fresh fruit packed in ice and shrimps packed the same way. "You have enough shrimp here for an army. Wherever did you get such huge ones?"

"I know that prawns are one of your favorites, so I had them flown in for us. The soup is lentil and there is Jewish black bread."

Derry's mouth watered. "Ummmmm. Let's sit down." She felt real hunger for the first time since she and Aaron had separated. For months she had lived on fresh fruit and cheese, not wanting to cook. Sometimes she had gone for days without hot food. She had lost weight right away and continued to lose it.

They finished the tureen of soup and the round loaf of black bread. The small mountain of shrimp soon was whittled away, Derry murmuring with delight at every mouthful. She opened her mouth readily when Aaron offered her shrimp from his fork, the hot sauce dribbling down her chin.

"You're such a baby, Derry." Aaron leaned over and let his tongue clean the sauce from her chin.

When their eyes met, she steeled against the shuddering sob rising up in her. She bit into her lip until she could taste blood.

Aaron frowned at her. "What is it, love? Why are you so tense all at once?"

"I hope the children are all right." She swallowed hard, then jumped to her feet. "I had better check." She reached for the steam cart. "I can take this to the kitchen, too."

"We'll both go." Aaron rose, stacking the dishes on the cart with careless abandon. "Then we'll have our coffee and cognac up here." He grinned at her. "I asked Jim to make some of those special eclairs of his that you like so much."

"Oh, don't tempt me. . . . Jim? Did you say that Jim is here?" Derry had a sudden desire to see the man who had come to be a friend to her in the years of her marriage.

"Not tonight he isn't, but he'll be here tomorrow. He's coming with us."

"What will Jim do on the construction site at St. Thomas?" Derry frowned at him, trying to keep the poorly stacked dishes from falling off the moving cart.

"He'll be helping you in the house." Aaron pushed ahead of her into the small elevator, jostling the cart into position and pressing the "hold" button so that Derry could enter.

"There won't be much for me to do, will there? I could just as well stay here." Derry felt a hollow unloved feeling all at once.

"Don't be an ass, darling." Aaron leaned over the cart and kissed the corner of her eye. "You have to take care of me."

"I tried that once, and was told that I failed miserably."

"And I told you to ignore my family. They aren't important to you and me. Friends and family are secondary to us."

"I wish I could believe that," Derry muttered following at his heels. "Do the Weeks still work for you, Aaron?"

"Yes, but they're off for the weekend to see their daughter who lives in Connecticut." He started to dump the dirty dishes into the sink.

Derry pushed him aside, glaring at him. "You are still sloppy in the kitchen." She rinsed each dish and placed it in the dishwasher.

"No, I'm not. You're too fussy." Aaron grinned at her.

"And you don't realize how much work it is to clean encrusted food from dishes." Derry surprised herself when she poked her tongue at Aaron after pressing the "Rinse and Hold" button on the dishwasher.

Aaron threw back his head, a loud guffaw escaping him.

When Derry tried to get by him, two broad, strong hands manacled her waist.

"I have to punish you for that, devil doll." His mouth hit hers like a ram, forcing entry into her mouth, his tongue in loving pressure against her teeth and the roof of her mouth.

Derry pulled back from him. "Children," she said in a mock-serious warning tone.

"All right, Mama, we'll check on our children." He smiled down at her. "Now we have a family at last, Derry. Are you happy?"

A sharp pain rose in her middle, yet she managed to smile back. "Yes. The children have made me very happy. After the first week, I wondered what I had ever done without them. They fill all the nooks and crannies of my life."

"They are great kids. Sandy and Dev did a good job."

"Yes." Derry expected a wrenching sensation to come with the mention of Dev's and Sandy's names, but it didn't. Instead she felt a sudden solace and sureness deep inside her.

As they walked up the stairs and around the balcony hall that led to the children's wing, Aaron wrapped an arm around her waist, fastening her to his side.

They could hear the buzz and chatter of Kim's and Sara's voices and the occasional murmur of Lee's before they entered. The day's string of surprises must have them so excited, Derry thought, that exhaustion must have not yet set in. Then, too, they had slept so much on the plane rides. The childrens' suite consisted of a sitting room with bedrooms on either side.

Sara and Kim charged at them as they came into the room, a smiling Lee maintained his dignity by walking to them.

"We have a trundle bed. Sara's to sleep in the crib, but when she's bigger she can sleep in the trundle. My bed is big. I have two pillows." Kim took a breath and smiled at Aaron. There was a gaping hole where a tooth should have been.

Aaron hunkered down in front of the child, one hand covering the side of Kim's face. "You've lost your tooth. Did you put it under your pillow?"

Kim grinned and nodded, eyes alight. "The tooth fairy will come tonight, Lee says. Will he, Da?"

Aaron was about to answer when he noticed Lee suck in his breath and Sara say "Is he Da?"

He nodded to Telford who nodded back and left the room. He lifted Sara into his lap and gestured for Lee and Kim to sit on the sofa next to Derry. He sat on the chair with the baby in his lap. "I'd like to be your Da, that's true." Aaron smiled at each one in turn. "But you must never feel that you have to call me that. All right?"

Kim and Lee nodded. Sara yawned. "I call you Da." She patted his cheek. "I sleep now. 'Huggy banky.' "

Aaron looked at Derry, puzzled, then watched Lee ferret the "huggy banky" from under some clothing in the suitcase that belonged to Sara. It was a tattered, parchment-thin scrap of material that, indeed, had once been a blanket.

Derry hugged and scrutinized each child in turn as Aaron did the same. The children smiled back sleepily and went to bed. Derry followed Lee from the girls' room, across the sitting room to his own bedroom. "Lee?" She cleared her throat. "Are you . . . is everything all right?"

He turned to her, wrapping his arms around her waist. "We'll be fine, Derry. Honest."

"Yes." She bit her lip to still the quivering. "Yes. You'll be fine."

"Good night, Lee." Aaron spoke from close behind her, his hand going out to clasp the boy's shoulder.

"Good night . . . sir." Lee folded back the top blanket to form a precise triangle, then climbed into the bed, allowing Derry to cover him and give him another kiss.

When she and Aaron were out in the hall once more, she paused.

"What is it, Derry?"

She shrugged. "It's silly, I suppose, with Telford here, but the children have had recurring nightmares about the death of their parents. At first I spent the whole night with them. I would like to stay here for just a while to see if they sleep." She looked up at him, feeling her pulse flutter. "I'll just wait in the sitting room for a time."

"We both will." Aaron took her elbow, leading

her into the children's room once more and whispering something to Telford, who was gathering socks and underwear and placing them into a string bag. She nodded and left the room. "So, now you can tell me about how the children came to call Dev 'Da.' "

Derry laughed as she took the straight chair, pretending she didn't see Aaron gesture for her to sit on the sofa. She ignored the satiric smile he gave her. "That was Sandy's doing. Her grandmother was Welsh and Sandy had always called her own father 'Da.' So it was a natural thing for her to pass on to the children."

Aaron was silent for a long while, his clasped hands dangling between his knees as he stared at her. "Did you really think that I would let you marry that fool, Derry? Did you actually believe that I would let that pompous ass near you?"

Derry ignored his questions. "I can imagine what Linda Lisman is thinking, what everyone in the town of Laneport is thinking at this minute." She covered her eyes with one hand, more to escape from Aaron's gaze than anything else.

"What do you care what people think?" Aaron leaned back on the sofa, letting his long legs stretch out in front of him.

Derry glared at him. "Laneport is a close knit community—and it's not at all like that gathering of arrogant twits compromising your family's circle of friends."

"Darling." Aaron leaned forward again. "You saw things that weren't—"

"Nuts!" Derry interrupted, feeling her throat tighten. "I can't remember how many times I was blinked at owlishly by the members of the Worcester Club, a look of horror coming over their faces as they would say, 'This is *really* the girl who married Lathrop's boy?' "

Aaron heaved a big sigh. "I didn't say that there weren't some people who were snobs. What I am saying was that you saw opposition at every turn, that your very self-consciousness invited that kind of—"

"Who wouldn't be self-conscious in that group?" Derry responded, more stung by his words than she would have liked to admit. "You were never treated in that fashion by my family."

Aaron shook his head, his teeth snapping together. "You damn well didn't have to take everything to heart. How many times did I tell you to ignore the people who were impolite to you?"

"Easy to say. They never treated you in such a fashion." Derry sniffed, lifting her chin, the uneasy feeling seeping through her that her former staunch arguments were grounded on quicksand.

"Derry, listen to me, please. I never had trouble with your family and friends in Laneport because I was willing to meet them halfway. You refused to do so with my family."

Derry surged to her feet, arms akimbo, jaw thrust foward. "Are you saying that it was my fault that your family was so supercilious to me? Because if you—"

Aaron rose from the sofa to grasp her upper arms. "No, I'm not."

"Why are you fighting?" Kim's lip quivered as she scrubbed at her eye with her fist.

Quarrel forgotten, both Derry and Aaron turned toward the distressed child.

Aaron reached her first and scooped her up into his arms. "Lots of mommies and daddies argue, lamb. That's the way it is in marriage, but it doesn't mean anything bad." Aaron hugged and kissed her, then placed his free arm around Derry's waist, bringing her close to the child and himself. Then he leaned down to kiss Derry gently on the mouth.

Derry let herself respond to the soft caress, her body leaning on Aaron. "That's true, love." Derry swallowed trying to steady the quaver in her voice. "We're a family." She leaned up to kiss the child, remorse filling her as she noticed the palpable relief on Kim's face as they talked to her.

"I'm tired." Kim yawned, relaxing in Aaron's hold as he walked back into the child's bedroom, put a finger to his lips as he looked at the sleeping Sara. He placed Kim into her bed and stepped back to let Derry cover her. Then they both kissed the child again and left.

They walked in silence toward their own wing, Derry's back stiff, her smile wooden as they passed Telford returning from the laundry room.

Once inside their own suite, Derry whirled on him. "See! What did I tell you! We can't get along for two minutes without arguing . . . and that is not good for the children."

"All right." Aaron spat the words at her. "Then from now on we don't argue."

"Ha!" Derry exhaled a whoosh of air. "That will be the day!" Her body thrust forward, aggression in every line.

His body mimed hers as he stared at her, his jawbone hard. "Yes, that damn well will be the day. This day. From now on we don't argue. We compromise." He thrust his hand toward her. "Agreed?"

Derry looked from his face to his hand and back again as though she expected spiders to leap from his body. She inhaled, then pushed out her hand. "It won't work, but I'll try."

"Damn you, Derry, for your hidebound Yankee ways. Stop being obstructive." He grasped her hand. Instead of releasing it, he gave it a slight jerk, catapulating her forward into his arms. "Is this the only way that I can control you? By making love to you?"

"You can't control me!" Derry said staunchly.

All at once, the frown on his face softened into laughter. "You're right there. More often than not you always controlled me."

"What?" Derry asked in a squeaky voice. "What a whopper that is! No one tells you what to do, Bostonian Boss Man." She pushed back from him, freeing herself.

"Name calling, wife?" Aaron drawled.

"Don't be ridiculous." She turned away from him so that when she spoke again, her back was to him.

"Get dressed, Derry. We're going out for a while."

Derry whirled around to stare at him. "No. I'm going to bed."

Aaron's eyebrows arched. "If that's what you want, devil doll. It certainly suits me."

"I meant alone, and you know it."

The angles and planes of Aaron's face had a geometric toughness. "We go together, angel—bed or out."

Derry swallowed, staring at him for long seconds. Had he always had that "carved-from-ivory" look about him?

"Stop staring, Derry, and tell me what we're doing this evening. Bed? Or out?"

"Out," she managed to say through stiff lips. She walked into the bedroom feeling the angry quiver in her knees. *Someday someone is going to tip you off the top of the World Trade Center, Mr. Aaron Thomas Cabot Lathrop III,* Derry thought grinding her teeth.

She pulled clean underthings from the dresser and stalked into the bathroom, still muttering angrily to herself. *And I,* she grated into the mirror at the person foaming at the mouth with tooth-paste, am going to end up gumming my food if I live with that man very long. I can't speak to him without grinding my teeth. It will serve him right if I get a pair of ill-fitting dentures and click clack at him all day. She rubbed moisturizing cream into her skin. It would serve the bastard right if I handed him a whopping fat bill for new teeth! She threw down her towel in disgust. I must be going out of my mind—actually looking forward to losing my teeth so that I can bill Aaron for the dentures.

She stormed back into the bedroom, almost wishing that Aaron was there instead of in the other room so that she could crown him with one of the Ainsley lamps that sat next to the bed.

Her evening suit was a Chanel jacket and pencil slim skirt in pearl blue silk that was a shade lighter than her eyes. The round buttons were crystal and she wore diamond studs in her ears and a diamond watch at her wrist.

Aaron knocked once and entered from the sitting room. His eyes seared her from head to toe, lingering at her ankles, then quickly returning to her face. "You're lovely. I hope that jacket comes off. We're going dancing."

"It does, but I won't need to take it off." Derry kept her chin up, her eyes meeting his.

"No? We'll see."

She did not question where the Rolls Royce came from. But she did compliment the smooth-ness of the ride from the apartment to the little club in mid-Manhattan called, simply, "Dane's." Aaron helped her to the sidewalk then whispered an unintelligible message to the driver before guiding Derry down the steps and into the darkened interior.

Derry tried to smother the flash of irritation

that coursed through her when the *maitre d'* stepped forward and said that it had been many weeks since he had seen Mr. Lathrop.

"This is my wife, Tom. Darling, meet Tom."

"Hello." Derry kept her voice level, but her blood bubbled when she heard Aaron chuckle as he took her arm and followed Tom.

"I was here with some members of my family, devil doll," Aaron hissed as he slid beside her into the small booth.

"I really don't care." Derry kept her nose in the air, cursing the feeling of relief that filled her.

Aaron ordered without asking her what she wanted, then turned to smile at her, his gaze piercing her pores, running through her veins, x-raying her mind. "Don't forget our truce, darling."

"I think I'll have a double scotch instead of the Saratoga Water and lemon," Derry said, and she gestured to the waiter who had been about to turn away.

"What?" Aaron growled the word into her ear. "You don't drink anything but a little wine or champagne."

"Bring the scotch, please." Derry smiled at the waiter.

"Angel, if you slip under the table, I'll join you there and we can start a new supper club fad— making love under the table." Aaron's voice was a purr, but his green eyes were marble hard, and his Harvard accent was pronounced.

"I don't know what you have to be angry about," Derry began, not looking at him. "I simply ordered a drink."

Aaron leaned back from her, one side of his mouth lifted. "You've always known right away when I'm angry, haven't you?"

Derry turned away, watching the gyrations of the dancers to the beguine beat.

"You've never been a drinker." Aaron frowned at her, as the waiter set the frosted glass in front of them.

Derry stared at the glass Aaron was lifting to his mouth. "No doubt that is root beer, instead of the usual Jameson's with ice." She lifted the glass in front of her and took a mouthful. She had the sensation of her teeth being cleaned before she began to swallow. Her inner lips burned, but she forgot that as her throat caught fire, the incendiary liquid passing into her stomach and becoming a conflagration. She fought the cough as heat rose into her neck and face. "Smooth," she croaked, blinking to dry up the tears in her eyes.

Aaron tipped his glass into his mouth, his eyes fixing on her as though his stare could nail her to the chair. "Take it easy," he growled at her.

"I am taking it easy." Derry sipped now, wishing that she had Saratoga Water and lemon. She blew cooling air over her lips and thought it wasn't quite as bad this time.

"We'll dance," Aaron said, rising to his feet and pulling her with him.

"Don't you ever *request*?" Derry hissed, trying to pry his fingers from her arm.

"With you it's a waste of time," Aaron stated, his tone bland as he swung her to face him, then wrapped his arms around her body, almost lifting her from the floor. "This is where you belong and where you will *always* belong."

"Bossy, arrogant man," Derry said, her own arms curling round his neck as her pulse kicked into overdrive. There was no way to calm herself, to keep aloof from him. There never had been a way for her to resist his incredible sexuality. In minutes she felt like an overcooked noodle draped against him, her heart pumping blood in double-quick time. She took short, quick gulps of air, hoping the added oxygen might cool her overheated emotions.

They danced to a faster beat, then a slower one, then elected to return to the table for something to drink. The scotch seemed tastier to Derry now that the ice had melted in it.

Aaron excused himself for a moment. While he was gone, the waiter returned. Derry ordered the same all around and smiled at the man.

She was sipping the fresh drink, trying not to grimace when the straight scotch hit the inside of her mouth. She wondered, in a detached way, how anyone could be a dedicated drinker. She found Saratoga Water far more palatable. On the other hand, she mused, she couldn't recall when she'd felt so relaxed. Perhaps in small doses, like she was taking it, booze could be salubrious. She giggled at the thought.

"I'll be blue damned! Is that another drink, Derry?" Aaron reached for the glass in her hand as he seated himself.

She pulled it out of his reach, sloshing some of the liquid down the side of the glass, some splashing on her dress. "Ohhhh. Stupid, Aaron." She chuckled. "Now look what you've done." She waggled her index finger in his face. "Tsk, tsk, tsk. Naughty, naughty."

"We're leaving." He glared at her as she cradled her chin in her hands and grinned at him.

"Aaron, darling," a woman caroled as she sailed up to their table in a cloud of chiffon and Joy perfume. Her guinea-gold hair gleamed in the candlelight as she took hold of the rising Aaron and planted a kiss full on his mouth. "You haven't called me in ages. Whatever have you been doing with yourself? We expected you at Churchill Downs, darling. It was deadly dull without you."

"How are you, Selene?" Aaron smiled down at the woman.

Derry stared at the tableau and wondered what the blonde would do if she, Derry, upended the rest of her scotch down her cleavage, which reached almost to her navel.

"I would like you to meet someone, Selene." Aaron turned the woman toward Derry, his smile slipping as he saw Derry surge to her feet, swaying just a tad.

"Yes, indeed, Aaron introduce me to Selene. Then she must tell me where she gets her hair colored. 'S a marvelous job." Derry blinked when the other woman gasped. Then she took a deep breath. "I think Aaron is shy about introducing me, but I'm not shy. I'm his trick for the night. One thousand dollars worth. So you can see that I'm not a cheap trick." Derry swept past the open mouthed Selene and the grim-faced Aaron, heading for the door. Her exit would have been pure Bette Davis if the floor hadn't heaved under foot causing her to bang against a table.

Over the buzzing in her ears she heard Aaron's mutter as he grasped her round the waist and propelled her toward the exit. "We're leaving together, Salome."

Five

Derry was grateful to Aaron for entertaining the children after the plane left Kennedy International. She adjusted the ice pack so that it rested more firmly over her left eye.

"Sinus problems, Derry?" Jim Sagawa bent over her, a cup of steaming tea in his hands.

Derry gritted her teeth when she heard Aaron's bark of laughter from across the aisle where he sat with Sara on his lap and Kim and Lee at the table opposite him. They were playing Uno. "Ah, not exactly. I rarely get headaches." She smiled feeling a knifelike jab behind the bridge of her nose.

"Here, drink this tea. It has lemon in it. No sugar." Jim smiled at the children across the aisle and then sat down next to Derry.

"She told Selene Drury that she thought she had a very good dye job on her hair," Aaron drawled, shifting the baby on his arm as Sara lay there, content to suck her thumb.

Jim's body jerked as he guffawed, and he spilled some of the hot tea on his hand. "Ouch!" He grabbed Derry's ice pack and pressed it against his hand. "You shouldn't make me laugh when I'm drinking tea, old son," Jim admonished, still chuckling. "Did she *really* say that to Selene?"

"Just drop the subject," Derry said, yanking back the ice bag from Jim.

Aaron ignored her. "Yes, she did. And she said a few other choice things that—"

"Aaron," Derry hissed, looking at him around the ice bag. "It isn't necessary to regale the children with some modern tales from Sodom and Gomorrah," she said, her voice firm. When both Jim and Aaron chuckled, she glared at each in turn, then looked out the window and closed her eyes.

She must have slept deeply because her next awareness was of Aaron shaking her and telling her they had just landed. "What?" She blinked up at him as he unhooked her safety belt. "So soon?" She sat up, swallowing several times in an attempt to irrigate her desert-dry mouth. The scenery flashing past the window looked amazingly like that in Bermuda. She looked back at Aaron, as he told Lee that he would unhook him as soon as the two bell warning sounded from the pilot's cabin.

"Why is Derry unhooked?" Kim caroled, drawing the eyes of the other two children to their aunt.

Derry grinned at Aaron, seeing his sudden discomfiture. "Yes, Da, explain that."

Aaron shot her an angry look then looked back at the children. "I made a mistake. I should not have unclasped my belt or Derry's. It's always wise to wait for the two bell signal."

Sara patted his cheek as he unclipped her and lifted her as the bell sounded. " 'S'awright, Da."

"Aunt Derry says that we learn from our mistakes," Lee said.

"Does she now?" Aaron shifted the baby in his arm so that he could take Kim's hand after gesturing to Jim to get the "huggy banky," which Sara was pointing to over Aaron's shoulder. "Let's hope she does . . . learn from her mistakes, that is." Aaron chuckled as Derry glared at him and threw the ice bag onto the table with a splat.

She was so busy answering Lee's questions, glowering at Aaron's back, and directing Barrow and Jim not to forget anything as they deplaned, that she didn't take notice of the long walk from the plane to the airport lounge. She looked around at the British and American flags. She was about to mention this oddity to Jim, when she realized they were going through customs.

Then they were on the sidewalk, and the cool breeze from the ocean was a welcome adjunct to the hot sun.

"Aaron . . ." Derry paused, frowning at the people around her.

"Never mind, Derry, here are the cars. We'll have to separate since these island cars are so small. I'll take Sara and Kim with me. Jim you ride with Derry and Lee. Barrow, you come with me."

"Oh, but . . ." Derry blustered, angry that Aaron didn't even look at her. She was still glaring his way when the car pulled away.

"C'mon, Derry. Let's go," Jim urged, then turned to say something to the driver, who nodded.

Derry found herself wedged in the back with luggage balanced precariously behind her. She wanted to say something to Jim, but he and Lee were engrossed in a question and answer session on cars and racing.

She sighed and looked out the window, uneasiness building in her as they passed a naval station then crossed a causeway. Derry's mouth dropped as she saw the sign that said "St. George's." Before she could say anything the car whipped around a curve and up a hill, upsetting some of the valises and dumping them onto her head. She started to laugh when she saw Lee's concerned face peeking at her through the mess. She chuckled even more when she heard his relieved laughter. She forgot to say anything about their location as Jim teased her about being buried under a mountain of luggage.

It was when they sped up the curving, crushed stone, hibiscus-lined drive that Derry knew for certain they were in *Bermuda*, not St. Thomas. She could never forget Windrift, the home that had belonged to Aaron's maternal great-uncle, the place where she and Aaron had honeymooned, where the semitropical splendor isolated them from the world.

Mouth open, lips trembling, insides separating into painful chunks, Derry stared at the pink stucco house with the white lime roof, the green shutters like open arms at every window, the sweep of front stairs to the circular drive like an entrance to a Mayan pyramid. Even the doorway had an unusual touch to it. The lintel flared in oriental grace as though in elegant greeting.

Derry's teeth began to chatter as the small car chugged up the remainder of the hill and jerked to a stop in front of the steps. Lazslo, in white coat as always, beamed at her. He opened the car door and jerked his head at his minions to see to the luggage.

"You honor us, indeed, Madame Lathrop. Lo, how we've missed you." The clipped British accent seemed strange coming from the mouth of

SURRENDER • 75

one who would have looked more at home on a brigantine with a skull and crossbones as the banner. Even though Derry knew Lazslo to be a superior houseman, she had to smile at the incongruity of the man's looks.

"It never ceases to amaze me, Lazslo, how out of costume you look without a sword." Derry managed to keep her voice steady and stiffen the rubber in her smile.

Lazslo's smile broadened on his *café au lait* colored features. "My ancestor, Captain Hezekiah Frith would be relieved to know that one of his descendants at least looked the part, madam, though he is only a houseman and not a member of the Brotherhood of Pirates."

Derry placed her hand on the white coated arm. "Not just a houseman, and you know it, but the best houseman in the world. So said Sir Rupert the last time I spoke to him before he passed on."

Lazslo blinked several times and swallowed. "You are kind, madam, as always." He took a deep breath. "I can only be glad that Sir Rupert deeded Windrift to Master Aaron." He inclined his head toward the children who had slowly gathered around Derry and were looking upward at the tall, handsome Bermudian with the curling white hair. "Ah. And so you are the young master and young ladies." Lazslo didn't notice Derry's openmouthed, shocked look as he shepherded the youngsters up the wide fan-shaped lime stairs to the house. Jim trailed them.

"Close your mouth, darling. You'll catch flies." Aaron loomed over her, his mouth descending like a jack hammer, his tongue intruding into her mouth like a velvet knife.

Derry pushed back from him, gasping. "Stop it. People."

Aaron folded her closer, his mouth gentle this

time. "I've got you now, in my own Bluebeard's castle." He shook his head slowly. "You'll never get away from me again." Aaron nipped at her face from ear to ear. "I'm loving you from now until you're ninety . . . and beyond." Aaron's laugh had a thread of steel woven through it.

"I'll get tired," Derry said in hazy fashion.

"Then I'll make sure that you get lots of good food and rest in this paradise."

"This isn't St. Thomas." She rallied to the attack.

"God, you're a bright one." Aaron chuckled, easily holding her arms when she struggled.

"Lizard," she said hotly. "Don't you patronize me!"

"Feisty brat!"

"Why did you bring me . . . us here?"

"Don't you think it's beautiful?" Aaron turned her in his arms, still keeping her manacled to his body, to look out over the ocean across the South Channel. Here and there thrusts of white sandy beach pushed their way into the turquoise depths.

"Yes." She gulped, feeling his heart thud against her back. "It has God's own beauty in every nook and cranny."

"This is where it all began for us." He leaned down over her shoulder, breathing the scent of her hair. "Now it begins again. And this time, nothing will separate us. I'll see to that."

"You're an arrogant, opinionated man who comes from an autocratic family that undoubtedly *thrived* in the Dark Ages."

"We did thrive in the Dark Ages, darling," Aaron crooned.

"Naturally! Your family chief, Attila the Hun, drank himself to death, too, I've heard."

Aaron's chuckle rumbled at her neck, his hands tightening at her waist. "Sorry, love, we can't take credit for him. One of my relatives probably taught Attila everything he knew, though."

"True." Derry tried not to smile, but she couldn't tear the picture of Aunt Sylvie shaking her finger in Attila's face from her mind. Besides, leaning back on Aaron's broad chest was so comforting.

"Come along, I want to show you our room."

"I've seen our room."

"No, not this one, you haven't. I've had the master suite redone."

They walked through the house. Aaron waited patiently while Derry stopped to run her hands over the Sheraton desk of burnished mahogany and then the piecrust table of gleaming rosewood.

"I have always loved these pieces." She looked up at Aaron. "Is the library just the same? With the wall-to-wall books and the handmade lace drapes from Madeira?"

"Yes." Aaron's eyes had a velvet glitter to them. "You remember so much that I'm encouraged about my terms of unconditional surrender."

Derry stiffened. "What does that mean? Because if you think that I will—"

Aaron leaned down and kissed her nose. "Forget that. I'm going to show you our suite of rooms."

Whenever Derry would broach the subject of "surrender" on the way up the stairway that hugged one curved white wall, Aaron would stop and kiss her and murmur "not to worry."

Derry worried. She had the nagging suspicion that she had stepped into quicksand again and that if she wasn't alert she would disappear into the Lathrop power and lose control not only of her own life but of the children's as well. She was about to confront Aaron with this when they reached the double doors leading to the suite, the ornate gold leaf trimming it having a rich gleam.

Aaron threw open both doors and urged her forward.

Derry sucked in her breath at sight of cream and beige elegance. Turquoise and blue touches in the pillows and cushions augmented the beauty of the bedroom. The room belled out in a semicircle. The rounded part was all glass with a door in the middle leading to a white painted deck, which repeated the bell shape out over the craggy ground that spilled onto the sandy beach and the ocean. The door was open and a soft breeze rustled through gently interfering with the calm perfection of the room. "It's lovely," she whispered, afraid to spoil the moment.

Without speaking, Aaron led her across the ankle deep champagne colored carpet to the mirrored wall. He pressed a button and the mirrors slid back to reveal a mile of clothing: suits, long and short dresses, robes, slacks, jeans, shorts. Derry looked at Aaron, puzzled.

"Your wedding present, love. I had your friend Clorida design some things you'd need for this climate and send them. Come. I want you to see our sitting room."

A little dazed, but still wary, Derry let him lead her in to a door in the opposite wall. At one side of this was a small escritoire, the blue enamelled surface the exact color of one of the throw pillows. Derry touched it. "Louis XIV?"

Aaron shrugged. "Could be. When Jim and I came down here to do this suite over, we found a warehouse full of stuff like this in the old carriage house. Lazslo was delighted when we decided to use what we could. I remembered how much you like antiques."

Derry stopped and turned to look at him. "When did you do all this?"

"Do you like it?" Aaron pushed open the door and turned her to face the sitting room.

"Aaron! Oh, Aaron! It's—it's perfect." Derry sighed and moved forward into the room with it's cream-colored satin couch and side chairs grouped in front of a rounded brick fireplace. A circular, gold leaf coffee table was the focal point of the grouping of furniture. Here the accent colors were rose and soft pink in the throw pillows. The effect with the champagne-colored carpet was warm and inviting.

"There's another, smaller bedroom on the other side of this room that I'm sure was used as a nursery." Aaron looked around the room, a satisfied smile on his face. He didn't see Derry bite down hard on her lower lip. When he looked back at her, her face was expressionless. "Well?"

"It's lovely and I like it very much, but you didn't say when you had done all—"

"Over a period of time," Aaron said in a clipped voice, not looking at her. He threw open the door on the other side of the sitting room. The cream and champagne colors were accented with shades of green ranging from lime to forest. Twin beds sat at right angles to a bevelled rosewood armoire that gleamed in the sunlight streaming in the window. "There's plenty of room for us to move around, as you can see." He turned to look at her, a frown on his face. "Why are you smiling?"

"After nine years of marriage, there are still things about you that surprise me. I knew you were a construction man, but I didn't know you were into interior decorating." She laughed. "What I wouldn't have given to see you with paint daubs and fabric swatches!"

"You wouldn't have seen it," Aaron snapped, blood running up his neck. "I told them what I wanted. If it wasn't right, they took it back."

"Of course." Derry turned away, disappointment snaking through her for some reason.

"You'd probably like to shower before dinner." Aaron was aloof all at once.

"Yes." Grouch, she thought and sailed past him into the bedroom. He followed. She whirled to face him. "You *did* say that there were two bathrooms with this suite?"

"No I didn't say that, but it happens there are two." Aaron's face had the same frozen look it had often had after they had had a fight. No, not a fight, just a teeth gritting word contest, Derry thought, glaring at him as he strode across the room and out the door, the heavy oaken door resounding like a kettle drum.

She didn't take a shower. Not when she saw the circular tub with the jacuzzi. She lowered herself into the swirling water that steamed from the cream-colored tile depths and admired the hand carved azuelos that decorated the wall from floor to ceiling.

She sighed and let the moving water lift and twist her body, remembering the time one August when Aaron had taken her to Saratoga Springs for the races. He had insisted that she take the baths and have the massage at the Roosevelt Baths, which were within walking distance of the Gideon Putnam Hotel where they had stayed. She smiled, her eyes closing, as she pictured how Aaron had waited for her, having finished first. When he saw her rosy glow, her relaxed face, he had rushed her back to their room. Instead of watching the thoroughbreds pound down the track, she and Aaron had lain naked on the bed, mouth to mouth, hip to hip . . . Derry shot up into a sitting position in the tub, sloshing some of the water over the sides.

She pressed her hands to her hot face. She could have sworn that she had forgotten all about that trip to the spa. God, she had to protect herself from Aaron. Her head jerked up, free of her hands. Fool! she castigated herself. How are you ever going to be free of him now? Why didn't you fight harder before caving in like a wet noodle and marrying him again? "I couldn't involve the children in a brouhaha." She laughed at the foolishness of that defense.

"Who are you talking to?" Aaron spoke from the doorway, a towel cinched at his waist, his bare shoulder propped against the door jamb. "You look very intriguing, wife, like Aphrodite rising from the bubbles."

"Don't be silly." Derry started to slide down into the bath again.

Aaron was beside her in one stride, his sinewy arms reaching down and lifting her straight up out of the water. He placed her on the carpeted floor, then enveloped her in a fluffy bath sheet.

"No," Derry gasped.

"No, what?" Aaron's grip tightened, folding her close to his body. "The children have had their dinner and want to walk on the beach before bedtime. I said we'd take them. Shall I tell them you don't want to go?"

"No." She tried to maneuver her hands free of the towel.

"You say 'No' too much, my lovely devil doll. I'm going to teach you to say 'Yes' . . . all the time."

"Don't bet your check on it," Derry snapped, grinding her teeth as the heat rose in her body at his closeness. "Hadn't you better get dressed?"

His mouth swooped, taking hers with his firm lips, penetrating and touching the sensitive roof of her mouth. He pulled back a fraction. "I love to taste you, wife."

"Mouths are for dental work," she shot back, trying to be scathing.

Aaron laughed, lifting her so that he could look her in the eye. "Let's debate the question."

"Are you playing games now? Aren't we going to walk on the beach?" Kim wailed from the door, holding Sara with one hand, Lee looking over her shoulder.

Aaron didn't release her as he looked toward the door. In fact he held her tighter. "Mommies and Daddies *do* play games together," he pointed out in gentle tones. "Come in."

Kim and Sara ambled forward, Lee hung back.

"Put me down," Derry hissed through clamped teeth.

"All right, but we have unfinished business. Don't forget it. I won't."

Derry knew red was staining her cheeks as she smiled at Lee to enter the room as well while clutching at the towel that was threatening to unwrap from her body.

"I told them that we should wait on the lanai," Lee said, enunciating each word carefully.

"No. No don't be silly." Derry took a deep breath, keeping a wary eye on Aaron who was crouched down in front of the two girls, whispering to them. "Just give me five minutes and I'll be ready. Sit down, my sweets." Derry grabbed underwear, cuffed shorts and a short sleeved shirt in hot pink and scampered for the dressing room, locking the door behind her.

When she returned to the room—not five but nine minutes later as Lee informed her, a glimmer of amusement in his eyes—Aaron was all ready and propped against the wall as though he had waited hours instead of minutes. All five of them enjoyed the game.

The Bermuda twilight was soft. The luminescent orange, purple and gold in the sky made the few early stars seem pale. The sand was shimmer-

ing silver in the fading light and cushiony under-
foot.

Sara, wide-eyed at the froth of waves throwing
themselves at the beach, clung to Aaron at first.
After a while, she pushed to be let down, still
clutching her "huggy banky" to her face, and went,
stumbling and staggering, to the water's edge.
The other two raced to the water's edge, too.

"They'll get wet and sandy." Aaron laughed. The
baby threw some sand in the direction of the
water, then turned to run back to him, chortling
at her achievement.

"Yes." Derry smiled, leaning down to open her
arms to the toddling child. "But what a wonderful
place for them to vacation. They'll have such a
wonderful time here." She looked up at Aaron but
he was watching a cruise ship go by, running
lights, deck lights and muted music giving the
illusion that the vessel was passing just in front
of them instead of a few miles out in the channel.

By the time they returned to the house, Sara's
head was nodding on Derry's shoulder and Kim
was asleep on Aaron's. The usually quiet Lee was
describing in great detail the purple, balloon-like
carcass of the Portuguese man o'war he had seen
washed up on the sand.

"And do you die from the sting?" Lee asked, a
mixture of fear and awe in his voice.

"Not from one," Aaron answered. "A school of
them could be real trouble. The sting is nasty."

Lee nodded his head even as he mouthed more
questions. "And we'll fish and everything?"

"And sail and swim and snorkle." Aaron was
solemn, but his eyes gleamed in amusement at
the boy's enthusiasm.

As they mounted the beautiful curving staircase,
their grand plans grew with each step. Derry felt
the sting behind her lids as she heard Lee really

open up for the first time. He had needed a father. He needed Aaron. Well, so do I, she moaned
to herself, almost blocking out the inner voice
that told her she was a fool for succumbing to
him again. I am not succumbing, she fought back
in her mind, even as she lowered the baby to
the sink in the girls' bathroom to sponge off the
sand.

Sara didn't even waken as Derry washed her.
Her soft mouth, parted in sleep, looked as lovely
as a rosebud. Derry hugged the rounded body to
her and kissed the child before lowering her into
the crib. Then she went to Kim's bed to give her
one last kiss. Kim's shakey smile told Derry the
child was almost asleep.

She stood in the doorway of Lee's room and
listened to the boy.

"Just tell me one more thing, please, then I'll go
to sleep. What kind of fish will we catch?" Lee
snuggled down under his light cover. The air con-
ditioning was turned off so that the ocean breezes
could blow through the room.

"Rock fish," Aaron answered at once, tapping
the boy on the nose. "Good night."

Lee took a deep breath and nodded. "Night . . .
and thanks. I like Bermuda."

"So do I."

When Aaron rose from the bed, Derry went forward. "Good night, Lee."

Lee's thin arms reached for her, clamping on
her neck. "I like Aaron a lot better than Gerard,"
he whispered.

She nodded, kissing him, then rose to leave,
aware that Aaron was still in the room and now
was waiting for her to precede him.

• • •

"Shall we have a nightcap on the lanai?" Aaron cupped her elbow, leading her out of the dining room where they'd just had a light dinner.

"I think I'll go to bed instead." Derry tried to pull free.

"Then accompany me while I have one. I want to speak to you." Aaron's voice had a strained sound to it. He didn't release her arm.

"Can't it wait until tomorrow?"

"No, it can't."

"All right. I'll come with you. But make it short. I want to get to bed."

"I'll be going to bed with you, devil doll." Aaron laughed.

She fought the hot tide that rose in her body at the thought of going to bed with Aaron, making love, sleeping in his arms. She clamped her teeth together, averting her eyes from Aaron's face as they descended the staircase to the lower landing that led to the lanai.

"To answer the question in those raised eyebrows—" Aaron leaned down and kissed her brows. "I have always loved the beautiful arch they have."

"You were saying?" Derry coughed to clear her constricted throat. She sank down into a white wicker chair upholstered in celery and green cotton. "So what did you want to talk to me about that couldn't wait until morning?"

"You heard Lee before? When he said that he liked Bermuda?" Aaron splashed Irish whiskey over some ice cubes and tossed some of it down his throat.

"Yes." Derry swung one leg in jerky cadence. Why was Aaron acting so ambivalent to her? "Yes. I heard him."

"Well, I believe that the girls are happy here, too. Jim and Barrow fuss over them and Telford is kind, but firm with them."

"That's a great deal of assumption for just one day of vacation," Derry shifted in her seat.

"This is more than a vacation, Derry."

She frowned at him. "What do you mean? Will you get to the point of this discussion?"

"All right." He wheeled to face her, tipping the rest of the whiskey to the back of his throat, then setting the glass down with a thump on the table between them. "We'll be living here for a while."

"What?" Derry leaped to her feet, arms akimbo, facing him. "What do you mean? We can only be here for a short vacation. I have a job, you know, and the children's spring vacation ends soon."

"I've been in touch with your employers and the school, and—"

"What? How dare you? You had no right." Derry's voice raised with each word.

"I'm your husband."

"But not my owner. I like my job. I'm good at it—"

"You're a mother with a mother's responsibilities," Aaron riposted. "That's a full time job, too."

"I know that. But when we get back it will be up to me to terminate my employment, not you."

"We're staying here for some time."

"The children? School?" Derry's voice was a mere croak.

"I enrolled them at St. George's Prep. They start on Monday."

Six

Windrift had been an armed camp since Aaron had made his disclosure to her three nights before. Even though she scarcely spoke to him when they were together, it didn't deter him from making love to her each night. She cursed her traitorous body, which turned to jelly at his touch; her mouth, which kissed him back; her arms, which held him close to her.

She heaved a sigh of relief as she looked out over the lanai, that belled out over the rough, downward slope of land to the ocean. Hibiscus bloomed in a riot of colors almost too strong for the eyes. Today Aaron had left for St. Thomas, Barrow with him.

This morning Telford would accompany her to the beach with the children. Jim Sagawa was coming with them, too, so that he and Derry could snorkle for a while.

Kim and Sara bounced with delight as they headed down the path leading to the beach.

"I usually don't like kids and I sure didn't want to come to Bermuda with you and Aaron." Jim looked at her, his gremlin smile widening. "But I like these kids. They're fun and they're smart."

"Is that because Kim called you wonderful yesterday?" Derry asked him.

Jim laughed. "Well, you'll have to admit the kid has good taste." He grinned at Derry, then set Sara on the blanket that Telford had spread for the children.

"Do you think it will be hard on them, Derry? Starting another school so soon after starting at one in the States?" Jim's face had a concerned twist to it.

Derry took a deep breath. "I've talked to both of them at length and they say that they love Bermuda and want to stay, but I'm still concerned about them starting today. The teachers tell me that it's best if I bring them at play time." Derry shrugged, biting her lip. "I'll be able to tell more after they return home." She rolled her jeans into a neat bundle and put them on the corner of the blanket, not taking her eyes from the three squealing children who charged the foaming waters and retreated from the breaking waves. "I'm not to pick them up. They have passes for the bus and I've been assured that the bus drivers will look out for them—especially since they are new." Derry handed the tanning lotion to Telford, who then returned to the children, the skirt of her bathing suit flapping wetly against her thighs.

"But you don't trust them, the drivers that is, to deliver our kids at the end of the drive. Oh, don't look at me like that, Derry. You don't even trust the stout-hearted Telford that much."

"Yes, I do," she protested to Jim, grabbing at her racing cap and getting to her feet. "Who knows.

I might not even be at the house when they return. I–I might be in Hamilton shopping."

"And would you like to borrow my moped instead of taking the bus? I have two nice carry baskets that can hold lots of parcels." Jim rose, following her to the water.

"Maybe I will." Derry cursed the bravado that was locking her into a trip into Hamilton she had had no plans—and no desire—to make.

She played with the children in the shallows for a while, then at Jim's and Telford's insistence she left them in their care to swim through the high, rolling turquoise water. As usual, the salt water massaged at her frayed edges. She swam out a distance, then turned and swam parallel to the beach, her breath coming in deep gasps as the water pummelled her body. When she felt the pull of a current, she realized that she was getting too near a grouping of rocks that Aaron had warned her about in previous years when they had made trips to Windrift as a married couple. She heaved her body around and swam back the way she had come, realizing that she had angled her stroke more into deep water. By the time she corrected and swam back to where Jim was treading water, she was breathing hard.

"I thought I was going to have to come after you, lady," Jim growled.

"I can out swim you any day." Derry gasped, laughing, knowing that Jim was almost as strong a swimmer as Aaron.

"Yeah?" Jim grinned at her, wading with her back into more shallow water where the snorkeling equipment waited, Lee standing next to it.

"Jim says that I might try snorkeling today. Can I, Derry?" Lee squinted at her.

She took a deep breath. "Well, I would rather Aaron was here with Jim, but I guess you could have a little early instruction." She grinned at the boy, who was slapping at his thighs in an unusual show of excitement.

Jim shrugged. "The big guy will have my eyes for this no doubt, but . . . ah what the hell? C'mon Lee, I'm better at this than Aaron anyway."

Lee looked solemn. "No, I don't think you could be as good as Da." The boy turned and walked toward the cluster of equipment near the water's edge.

Derry choked and her eyes filled with tears. Lee had accepted Aaron as his father! He had actually called him "Da." Her tears turned swiftly to laughter, though, as she looked at Jim. His mouth was agape as he stared after Lee.

"Tell me how the big guy does it, Derry?" He shook his head, a reluctant grin on his face.

She merely shook her head. Lee took to snorkeling like a natural, listening and absorbing every instruction.

To Derry's surprise, much of what Aaron had taught her came back, and she found herself relaxed and eager as she sought to follow Jim's movements.

When Jim was sure that Lee had had enough for the first time, he took Derry out into deeper water so that she was able to enjoy the beauty of the coral reef. She remembered how Aaron had warned her to use caution on the knife-sharp substance that was the skeleton of sea creatures, that a cut could be deep and dangerous.

After an hour Jim called a halt, telling her that she would be too tired if she went on much longer.

Derry didn't feel tired until she removed the equipment and lowered herself to the blanket near the children. Then the muscles in her legs began to quiver. She smiled at the baby, who was snoozing under the wooden canopy erected to provide shade. The screening on the sides protected Sara from the few bugs that were about.

Lee and Kim were busy digging trenches and moats around their sand castles. Jim watched them for long moments. Then, as though he couldn't help himself, he joined the children and was soon digging and building and packing wet sand as industriously as the children.

Derry was snoozing lightly when Telford sat down next to her on the blanket. Derry sat erect, blinking the sleep from her eyes.

"Mrs. Lathrop . . . ah . . . I know that you are very close to the children, but I wanted to tell you that I've grown fond of them too, even in the short time that I've known them. And I wouldn't let any harm come to them."

Derry could feel the heat in her face; it didn't come from the sun. "I know that Mrs. Telford—"

"Just call me Telford, please." The woman smiled. "It will make it easier for the children."

Derry smiled back, feeling a core of strain within her soften. "Your name is very like that of my husband's great-uncle Rupert Telbridge."

"Yes, I thought that. My name is English about four generations back."

By the time Telford rose to return to the screen enclosure where Sara slept, Derry felt reassured about the children's nanny.

Jim insisted on accompanying her when she took the children on the bus to St. George's Prep. Many of the children were in the schoolyard as they approached. Derry held her breath until two boys ran up to Lee and told him their names. Lee pulled a shy Kim forward with him.

A wide-eyed child with blond curls rioting over her head came up to Kim and said "Hallo" then giggled, clamping a hand over her mouth.

Derry gulped a sob as she watched. She was

glad for Jim's steadying hand as she went over papers with the principal then said goodby to the children who kissed her in a hurried way before rushing back to their new friends.

"Easy being a mother, huh?" Jim said, pressing a hankie into her hand as they waited for the bus.

"Awful." Derry sniffed, looking over her shoulder once more before she preceded Jim onto the bus for the short ride back to Windrift. Kim and Lee had disappeared with the others into the school.

An hour later Derry was assuring Jim that she had used a moped when she and Aaron had visited the island before. She didn't tell him that Aaron had let her use the bike only in the driveway when he was watching, and that when she went further afield, she had ridden on the back of Aaron's larger Harley Davidson with her arms locked around his waist.

Giving the worried Jim a cocky smile didn't stop the butterflies from rioting in her stomach as she coasted down the curving drive. She reached the narrow road that led to the main road to Hamilton without mishap. Wobbly at first, she gained a little confidence as she navigated the circuitous, somewhat hilly road, meeting walkers and a few other bikers. Everyone waved. At first Derry waved back, but the bike did such alarming things when she tried to manage it with one hand, that she merely smiled and nodded her helmeted head in greeting.

The main road leading to Hamilton was a different story. It was almost as narrow as the side roads and every bit as twisty. And Derry had forgotten about the buses that cannoned through the streets, sometimes just scraping round the walled thoroughfares! The hair rose on her neck when she heard one of the behemoths growl up behind her, the driver gearing down in irritation as he tried to go around her. When he finally did pass her, Derry could feel the pull of the larger vehicle against her body and her bike. Cold perspiration dribbled down the inside of her arm as she coughed exhaust fumes.

By the time she had travelled the three and more miles to Hamilton, she felt as though her hands had welded to the handlebars. Her eyes behind the plasticene goggles had a hot, fixed feel and she was wishing that she had done a bit more practicing with the bike before she had tackled the trip.

She forgot her worries after she stopped for an ice cream to bolster her spirits and freshen her dry mouth. She meandered through Trimingham's, Cooper's, into Pringle's, then along the main street to stare at a cruise ship disgorging its passengers. She watched the policewoman upon her traffic block, then went into the Irish Linen Store where she brought an embroidered, cream-colored linen cloth that would do nicely for the Sheraton dining table at Windrift.

She puttered along the street and back into the stores to study the displays of Belleek china, Waterford crystal, and myriad woolens and angoras. She found sweaters for each of the children in cotton cable knit and one for Aaron that was just the color of his sea green eyes.

She lost track of time as she studied the tartans. She bought skirts for the girls and plaid shorts for Lee and Aaron.

Her shopping bliss was shattered when she realized that she had much too much to fit into the carry baskets attached to the bike. She was nonplussed until she happened to look into the window of a sporting goods store and saw a large backpack of safety orange displayed in the window. It was the size that would hold a bedroll. Derry decided that she had solved her problem and went into the store and purchased it. The salesman obligingly helped her pack her parcels into it. Then when he saw how she staggered under its bulkiness, helped her fit it onto her back. He held her bike until she was started. He waved off the wobbly Derry with a smile. It wasn't too bad the first half mile, except her vision in her side mirror was somewhat obscured. She concentrated very hard on remaining on the left side of the thoroughfare and only drifted to the right twice.

She was halfway home when she began to feel the strain and pull at her shoulders. She tried shifting on the bike but it promptly wavered into the other lane.

She was still steadying herself when the Ferrari whipped around the curve coming in the opposite direction. She had a moment's sight of Aaron's goggle-eyed, openmouthed face before he was past her. She looked over her shoulder when she heard the brakes screech behind her and caught a glimpse of Aaron's car slewing around in a U-turn.

The blaring sound of the bus horn brought her head around and she realized that she had drifted into the wrong lane. She corrected just as the bus swept by her, the driver shaking his head.

Derry tried to keep the bike off the soft shoulder but she couldn't hold it to the road. The bike went down the shallow drainage ditch and up again, skidding into the loam of a freshly turned garden. Derry was thrown into the moist soil.

She knew she was unhurt in the soft, easy fall but her temper rose in rapid degrees as she struggled to a sitting position and looked at her parcels that had scattered from the backpack and were now clotted with mud. It was a relief to see she hadn't destroyed any of the young plants coming up in the good-sized garden. Although she had headed into the garden, the sudden stop in the soft soil had thrown her away from the plants and onto the weedy edge.

She yanked at her helmet as she staggered to her feet seeing Aaron come down the shallow embankment in jumps. The approach of a Bermudian, whom Derry assumed was the garden owner, was much more sedate.

"Derry! Derry, are you hurt?" Aaron threw himself at her, his arms outstretched.

Her hand shot out in front of her, her index finger accusing. "You—you clod. You—you obstructionist. You—you jerk!" She sensed that the Bermudian had paused in his forward motion. "You should be arrested! What are you trying to do? Kill me?"

Aaron stopped as though he had been pulled from behind, his eyes scrutinizing her form, top to bottom and back again. "Me? You were doing a damn good job of that on your own. Where did you learn to drive a moped? Kamikaze school?"

"What?" Derry clamped muddy hands on her hips, one hand still clasping the helmet strap. "Isn't that just like you? You philistine. You double-dyed road hog." She pointed to the wheel furrow that cut alongside the garden. "Just look at the damage to this garden, you criminal." Derry swiped one hand across her hot face then turned to look at the wide-eyed Bermudian who was staring from Aaron to Derry and back again. "If you decide to sue this vandal, I will be your witness."

"Oh, no, there is no—"

"Derry." Aaron grated out her name as though it were an oath.

"And what's more, I may sue you myself." She

thrust out her chin, then looked around with a yelp as she saw the sweater she had purchased for Kim coming halfway out of the bag. She bent down, edging it back into the bag with the heel of her hand. "I am definitely suing you. I hope they send you to Devil's Island." She continued to mutter and glare at him as he helped her retrieve her purchases.

"The French own Devil's Island, not the British. Besides that, it's closed." Aaron took the backpack from her. "You have a mud smear across your face."

"I'll get the French to reopen it and oil up the guillotine."

The Bermudian introduced himself as Dudley Warrington, retired. He brushed some of the caked soil off the bike and lifted it up. Aaron came forward to help the man but was waved away. "This is no trouble. I'm used to these things. There is no damage whatsoever, so please don't worry about it. I'm just happy the lady wasn't hurt."

Derry glowered at the solicitous man. "I'm sure the roots of something must be damaged. Shock, maybe."

"Not at all, not at all." The man smiled at them again when they reached the roadway, but Derry was still simmering and didn't notice, nor did she hear some of the exchange between the man and Aaron. "Oh, I understand," the Bermudian continued. "My wife is an indifferent driver too."

"What!" Derry whirled on the man.

Aaron took her arm above the elbow in an iron grip. "Let's go." He led her toward the Ferrari assuring the man that a friend would be along in a van to reclaim the moped.

The man assured them that that was fine and waved to them until they were out of sight.

"You hijacker." Derry ground out, gripping the

helmet on her lap, until her fingers ached. "You are an *atrocious* driver."

"Derry, if you ever pull a stunt like that again, I'll tan that round bottom of yours until it's bright red. I mean it."

"Don't you threaten me, bully. I intend to ride—"

"You will not ride that moped again until I say you are schooled enough on the side roads. I mean it, Derry. I forbid—"

"Forbid? Listen to me—"

"*I mean what I say.* Until I can get you a car, you can use the public transportation. The system is good, and it's safe."

Derry fumed. Silence carried them around curves, in and out of declivities. It surprised her when Aaron took the turn into St. George's but she clamped her lips together rather than ask his destination. He parked the car in an alley behind St. Peter's Anglican Church, turned to her, and wiped the dirt from her face with his handkerchief.

"I have to pick up a whiskey and wine order that Lazslo placed. Would you like to come with me? Or would you prefer to stay here?" Aaron's voice was cool.

She determined to stay in the car . . . even as she looked at the balmy breeze whispering through the royal palm tree in the churchyard, even as her eyes drank in the richness of the brightly colored houses that clustered on the hillside of St. George's. "I'll come with you," she muttered, opening her door and swinging her legs to the pavement before Aaron alighted from the car. She slammed the door behind her, not looking back.

Aaron took hold of her arm, shortening his stride to hers. "When are you going to stop fighting me, devil doll?"

"When hell freezes over." Derry gritted her teeth, trying to yank her arm free until she saw a man in gray clerical garb walking toward them down the alley.

He nodded and said, "Beautiful day."

Derry forced a smile onto her face. "Yes, indeed it is. Good day."

"My wife loves weather like this." Aaron smiled, too, at the cleric and put an arm tightly around Derry's shoulder.

"Release me," she hissed.

"Promise to behave? Promise?"

"Yes, yes." Derry shrugged away from him.

"Smile and I'll buy you an ice cream cone."

Derry felt her mouth twitch and her stomach rumble at the same time. "I'll take a chocolate milk shake."

They wandered slowly through the picturesque town, sipping milk shakes through straws.

Derry pointed to the wine shop but Aaron just shrugged.

"Let's get it on the way back. Let's go down to the wharf and see what vessels are here from the States."

Derry was agog at the many schooners flying American flags until Aaron reminded her that they were less than eight hundred miles from the coast of Carolina.

A tall blonde in braids, her D-cup overflowing the top of her bikini, waved at Aaron and lifted her eyebrows and beer stein in simultaneous invitation.

Derry wanted to tip him into St. George's Harbor when Aaron laughed, waved and shook his head. "How efficient of you to keep a stable," Derry observed, her smile Cheshire-Catlike as she stared across the bay.

"Temper, temper, devil doll. Whoa, take it easy. I can feel your blood heating from here. Come into

Trimingham's with me. I want to get something that I ordered."

Derry followed him, stiff outrage in every line in her body, her eyes drawing an imaginary target between his shoulderblades, her mind aiming one of the cannons of St. Catherine's Fort at the bull's eye.

Once inside the store, Derry had to pause to accustom her eyes to the dimness.

Aaron was gesturing to her, a little boy look to his smile. "Darling, how do you like it?" He pulled her forward, one arm going full around her as he inclined his chin toward the counter. In front of the smiling Bermudian woman waiting on Aaron was a tall Waterford lamp, the exquisite crystal refracting the colors around it.

"I love it, of course," Derry mused, her finger slipping out to touch the multifaceted surface.

"It's yours. Happy Anniversary." Aaron leaned down and kissed her open mouth.

"It's not our anniversary—for either marriage," she mumbled as he lifted his lips fractionally from hers.

Aaron chuckled, not releasing her, nodding to the woman to pack the lamp and send it to Windrift. "How could you forget the anniversary of the day we met? I thought men were supposed to be the black hats when it came to anniversaries."

Derry looked up at him, feeling her throat constrict. She couldn't have said anything to him if her life depended on it.

"I haven't forgotten," he whispered to her as he led her away from the counter, his arm around her, pausing in front of an array of gossamerlike wool stoles. He reached for one in a Bermuda blue, the muted turquoise color making her eyes glisten brightly as gems. "That's your color, devil doll." He looked up at the saleslady behind the

counter and indicated that he wanted the long
scarf.

When they left the store, they wandered up the
mall, looking into the windows of other shops but
not entering. Aaron had a firm grip on her hand,
his arm pressing her close to his side.

Derry didn't even rise from her euphoria when
Aaron informed her it was time to go home. The
children would be coming home on the bus soon
and he would like to spend a little time alone with
her first.

The sudden thickness to his voice had her heart
thudding in her chest. Her knees felt as though
someone had removed all the bones. Her breathing was out of sync as Aaron took her back to the
car, handed her into the front seat, joined her
there and in silence fired the ignition. Derry could
feel his pulse entering her as he shot the car
around the curves in the road leading away from
St. George's.

The curving entrance road to Windrift seemed
to come fast, and in minutes they were on the
private, white shelled concourse leading to the
house.

They left the car, still saying nothing.

Not even Laszlo was in the front hall as Aaron
lifted her and carried her up the curving stairs.
When they entered their suite, Aaron put her down
and shut the door, locking it.

"At last," he muttered, stalking forward, pulling
his shirt open, one of the buttons popping off the
material and disappearing into the carpet.

"Aaron, I . . ." Derry felt herself propelled forward by his hands, her body thumping up against
his chest.

"No talking, Derry. You scared hell out of me
today. If I think of what could have happened to

you in that accident, I'm apt to put you over my knee and whale you."

"Try it," Derry muttered, as his mouth feathered her cheek. "I'll punch you in the nose." She squealed as Aaron's breath fanned her ear.

"Little tiger." Aaron chuckled. His mouth closed over hers, marking her his, brooking no other opinion than that. His hands tremored over her body in spasmodic possession, the heat in them warming her from throat to navel.

"Won't the children be coming soon?" Derry asked in a detached way as Aaron pushed the shirt off her shoulders and unfastened her jeans.

"Not yet," he muttered hoarsely, his eyes fixed on her body as he peeled the bra from her skin. "I love your breasts." His voice was low but Derry felt each syllable throb in her blood. His hands skimmed lower and Derry felt herself divested of her panties, Aaron's mouth pressed to her abdomen.

Derry felt her eyelids grow heavy on her cheeks as Aaron rose with her in his arms. She sighed as the silken sheets on the bed caressed her back, her arms moving of their own accord to entwine at his neck.

"Love me, Derry, love me."

"Aaron."

"I like making love to you in the daytime," he muttered into her neck. "I love to look at your pink skin, your soft thighs . . . this . . ." He lifted his head to look at her, a slumberous look to him, as his hands made slow circular motions on the womanly part of her. When she gasped the blood rose in his face. "You're mine, Derry. You'll always be mine."

"B—bossy."

"Yes, my flower with the bluebell eyes." He rubbed her silky inner thigh.

"Aaron."

"Yes, angel? Do you like that?"

"Maybe." Derry bleated like a goat and Aaron chuckled. His hot breath feathered her skin as his mouth moved up and down her body in sensual concentration.

Derry felt a momentary rebellion that he could control her so effortlessly then she spiralled out of conscious thought, Aaron becoming her only anchor, her only reality. His body moved furiously with hers as he, too, scaled the sensuous mountain. The concerted explosion sent them off the peak together.

Long moments later, Derry was still clasped in her husband's arms, his one hand moving in lazy fashion from knee to neck and back again. Aaron had made love to her many, many times during their first marriage. In fact the first few years together, they couldn't be alone without the love erupting between them. Since the second marriage it had been much the same, even though with the children they were much more restricted. But the electricity was still there. Somehow, though, at this moment, Derry felt different. It was something elusive, something spectral running through her system, something that she couldn't describe.

"It's wonderful with us, isn't it, darling?" Aaron crooned into her ear.

Before she could answer her eye caught sight of the clock. "Oh!" She struggled free of Aaron's hold, sitting up quickly. "The bus." She swung her feet to the floor and was rising when he clasped her round the waist with one arm.

"What bus?"

"School will be out in two minutes. I want to be at the bus stop to meet the children." She strained against his arm. "I'm sure Sara will be up from her nap. I want to take her to meet Kim and Lee."

"I'll go with you." He pushed off the bed behind her, then swept her up into his arms. "Knowing you, you'll want a shower. When we first married, I was sure you would turn into a prune you bathed so much."

Derry kissed his shoulder, loving the feel of his bare flesh. "You take many more showers than I do." She felt herself slide down his body when he released her in the shower cubicle. "Aaron. Thank you for the lamp and the angora stole." She gulped at the hot look he gave her. "It was thoughtful of you, and I'm grateful."

"And I'm grateful for the gift you gave me, Derry." Aaron used the loofah on her back and the Joy perfumed soap with which he had stocked the bathroom. Besides the liquid perfume, there was also cream and body spray.

Feeling impish, Derry grabbed the soap and turned and rubbed it over his chest. He squalled and pushed backwards against the cubicle wall, making Derry laugh.

Even with the time-consuming job of drying her hair while listening to Aaron grumble as he showered again trying to remove the traces of Joy from his skin, they still weren't late.

Baby Sara gurgled with delight as she was carried down the curving, crushed white stone drive to the secondary road leading to Windrift property. When Aaron broke off an hibiscus, shook it to rid it of creatures and then handed it to her, she laughed.

"See. See. See." Sara shook the flower at Derry.

"It's beautiful, sweetheart. That hot pink color is just perfect for my baby," Derry cooed, reaching up to squeeze the dimpled knee at Aaron's neck.

"No baby. Big girl." Sara nodded emphatically.

Aaron laughed. "Watch it, Mommy. Didn't you know that we don't have any babies only bi-i-ig kids." Aaron turned his head and kissed the tiny leg on his shoulder.

Derry felt a wrench of exquisite tenderness as she watched the two of them, Sara's hands threaded through Aaron's thick dark blond hair, the child's eyes round as quarters as she looked around from her safe vantage point.

When they reached the foot of the quarter mile drive Aaron lowered the child to the ground, admonishing her to stay close to them and not to venture into the road.

All at once a mongrel shepherd, collie, beagle and the Lord only knew what else ambled by on the other side of the road. Sara froze.

The baby pointed, her high pitched voice like a clarion. "Myo, myo, myo." She lifted both arms to the dog, her lower lip trembling when the animal stopped, scratched his ear, and wandered on. Sara looked up at Aaron, pouting. "Myo." Her voice caught in her throat.

Derry bent down in front of her and hugged the child, looking up at the frowning Aaron to explain. "She misses Milo. She and the dog were inseparable."

Aaron nodded, hunkering down next to Derry, one hand almost covering the head of the child as he tried to comfort her. "I won't be able to get the dog here for a while. These things take time, but I have people working on it."

"You have?" Derry looked at him, surprised.

Aaron's smile had a twist to it. "Yes, Derry, I'm aware that our children need their pet."

The blood rose to her face. "I didn't mean that you would be insensitive to their needs, Aaron. I just didn't know . . . didn't realize—"

"Didn't understand me." The words sounded as

though they were punched out of his mouth. "No one knows that more than I do, lady."

"Aaron." Derry rose from in front of the baby, her hands stroking the baby's straight black hair.

Aaron looked past her, his face a carved mask. "Here comes the bus."

The driver eased the bus into the lay-by, his teeth gleaming in a smile as he watched Kim stumble off the bus talking, Lee following her, silent but smiling.

". . . And Da, we saw a bird's nest, and we got to touch the nest . . . and I saw . . ." Kim gulped a breath as Aaron pushed the hair back from her slightly damp forehead. ". . . and tomorrow I'm to bring a lunch pail and . . ."

Lee smiled at Derry. "We were fine." He looked at Aaron. "They have soccer—but they call it football—and cricket."

"We can practice on the lawn." Aaron grinned down at the boy. "Even though I can't be sure how good I'll be at cricket."

Lee grinned back. "I'll teach you."

Derry caught her breath watching them. She had never seen Lee so relaxed, so off the alert as he was with Aaron. With Sara on Aaron's shoulder they wended their way slowly up the path.

". . . and there are no bullies like Timmy Dearborn, I don't think." Kim's face screwed into a thoughtful frown, then cleared. "Marybelle Wilcox's cat has kittens and she says that I may have one."

Aaron turned as he walked and looked at the little girl. "And did your friend Marybelle say when the kittens would be weaned from their mother?"

Kim stopped, staring saucer-eyed at Aaron. "Are we to have a kitten, Da?"

"Kitty," Sara said.

Lee stared from Derry to Aaron, saying nothing.

"What do you think, Mommy?" Aaron gave her a lopsided grin.

Derry looked from face to face. "I think what Windrift really needs is a cat. You just never know when the mice will try to take over the world."

Kim squealed. Sara clapped with delight as she watched her sister jump up and down. Lee inhaled deeply, swallowed and gave Aaron and Derry a shaky grin.

Seven

Tom E. Cat was a ball of white and gray fluff with snapping blue eyes that, Lazslo assured the children, would turn to gold.

The children would lie on their stomachs for hours and watch the antics of the kitten with a spool of thread, a small rubber ball, a plastic mouse.

Jim Sagawa was scathing in his comments when the hapless creature pulled threads on his new cable knit pink cotton sweater. "If it weren't for the kids, I would drown that twirp," he muttered to Derry, his eyebrow crowded over his eyepatch as he watched the antics on the patio.

Two days later when Tom E. came up missing and the children were wailing, it was Jim and Barrow who combed the grounds while Lazslo tore the house apart.

When Jim found Tom E. sleeping under an hibiscus, he cuddled it to his chin, reluctant to hand it over to an eager Kim. He looked up to see

Derry watching him and shrugged. "Can't have the kids upset."

"No, of course not." Derry smiled at the red-faced man.

School went well for Lee and Kim, especially when Lee made the soccer team and both he and Kim discovered the Wendell twins, Archer and Ann. Though Ann was two years older than Kim, the placid youngster seemed a perfect foil for the ebullient younger girl. The foursome grew closer and closer, and not a day went by that some mention was not made about the twins.

When a car drew up one morning in front of Windrift to disgorge the Wendell children for a day with Lee and Kim, Derry made sure she was there to introduce herself to Mary Wendell.

"Our kids seem to be close." Mary's blond curls glistened in the hot Bermuda sun.

"Yes." Derry smiled back. "Why don't you stay for a while? We could have a picnic, swim."

Mary looked crestfallen. "Oh I wish I could, but I have an appointment to have my hair cut. Could I take a rain check, as you Yanks say?"

"Any time."

"Wednesday?"

"Great." Derry smiled and waved until the other woman was out of sight at the curve on the driveway.

Wednesday was a typical Bermuda day, balmy and sunny. Derry inhaled with satisfaction as she watched the Wendells come up the drive in the coughing Volvo.

Lazslo had told Derry he would bring all the things to the beach that they would need, including a cooler with drinks and another cooler with salads. Of course there would be cheese and crackers for snacks, but, here he frowned down at the children, no junk foods. There would be fruit and cheeses.

"Lazslo," Derry gasped when she saw him cart out boxes of food to load into the mini station wagon that he used. "We aren't going for a month."

Lazslo straightened from the back of the wagon and looked at the four eager children facing him. "No, madam, you are not going for a month, but children do get hungry."

"That puts you in your place," Mary muttered, standing closely behind Derry.

Derry put her hand to her mouth, stifling a laugh, and nodded to Lazslo.

Sara toddled over to Lazslo with Tom E. Cat in her chubby arms. For a reason known only to Tom E. he never scratched Sara when she picked him up and carried him, though he had been known to swipe at anyone else. "Cat," Sara burbled to Lazslo.

"No, no, Miss Sara. We must leave Tom E. at home. We would not want him lost, now would we?" Lazslo spoke in the usual soft tone he used with the children.

Sara shook her head, the straight ebony hair bouncing around her face. She lifted the cat toward Lazslo, who took it with a bow, then handed it to Lee, telling the boy to put it in the pantry.

Derry was feeling quite warm; she was glad to begin the downhill trek to the white expanse of beach that was like a white lace edging to the turquoise water.

"Tired?" Mary asked her, calling to Ann to take Sara's hand.

"I guess I'm having a reaction to all this good weather." Derry shrugged, wishing her mouth didn't taste like the bottom of an old sock. "How long have you lived here, Mary?"

"For ten years. We came from England right

after we married when James received an offer from Bermuda Telephone Company. We've never been sorry."

"I should think you wouldn't be. England has weather as bad as our area." Derry laughed, wetting her dry lips and sighing with relief when she saw that Lazslo had placed some deck chairs under the wooden shelters. She had a sudden desire for shade and a cool drink. Once again she was grateful to Sir Rupert, who had placed the wooden shelters at scattered distances from the water. She was quite close to the children playing at the water's edge when she was under the shelter.

"Are you going into the water, Derry?" Mary looked at her quizzically as she removed her terry cloth jacket to reveal her plump form in an emerald green bikini.

"Oh yes, I am." Derry rose from the chair, expelling air from her lungs. "I guess I just feel more lazy today than usual."

Derry didn't stay in the deep water too long, feeling an unaccustomed lassitude, a heaviness in her limbs. Years of competitive swimming had taught her the folly of pushing the body beyond the norm, unless it was for training. She headed back into the shallow water, watching Mary play ball with Sara. She sank down at the water's edge, her arms outstretched to the gurgling child as she clambered onto Derry's knee.

"She feels braver about the water from there." Mary chucked the baby under her chin.

"I know." Derry smiled. "The only time she is truly at ease in the water is when Aaron has her."

"No wonder," Mary observed. "I thought my Jim was big, but your husband is quite something." She looked puzzled for a moment. "It's funny that you and he speak with different accents."

"He's from Boston. I'm from upstate New York.

The accents are very different." Derry nodded, feeling limp all at once.

Mary lifted the baby from Derry's lap. "Let's sit under the shelter again." She turned her head to look at the four children concentrating hard on building a sand castle. "They'll be fine here."

In minutes Sara was yawning and soon curled up on a corner of the blanket with her "huggy banky" clutched to her.

"Have you seen a doctor yet? Or do you think it's too early?" Mary asked, glancing from the almost sleeping child to Derry and back again. "It's a good time. Sara will be potty trained and Telford will be itching for another one."

"What are you saying?" Derry questioned, her voice fading.

Mary stared at her, frowning. "I'm sorry, Derry. Didn't you want me to know?" She grimaced. "I suppose you think I'm a busybody now. Believe me, I don't mean to be. I never thought you wouldn't want to talk about it."

"Mary, I don't think you're a busybody. But—but you must be wrong, if you're thinking what I think . . . No, it couldn't be."

"You mean you think you aren't pregnant? Don't be silly." Mary's brow crinkled then cleared. "That's right. You've never been pregnant. I always forget that. You seem like such a natural mother to these children." She shrugged. "Still, I would be very surprised if you were not pregnant. What does your calendar say?"

"Huh? To tell you the truth, I don't check it as much as I used to. Ah, it *has* been some time since I menstruated, but . . . No! It can't be. Not now. I didn't think I could. I'm twenty-seven." Words spilled from Derry's mouth.

"Twenty-seven is a fine age to start a family." Mary giggled.

Derry took deep breaths. "Yes, it is, isn't it?" She bit her lip. "I'll—I'll be a mother of four, and it's my first time."

"I think you're beginning to accept my theory . . . that you're pregnant, that is."

"I think I am too."

"What will your husband say?"

"I don't know." Derry whispered. What would Aaron say? Would he want another child? Would he ask her why she hadn't conceived before now? He had better not, she thought. I don't have the answer to that one myself.

The rest of the day was a pink blur to Derry. She felt groggy but good. The heaviness was replaced by a funny lightness. The feeling of sand running through her fingers had an ethreal quality to it. The heat of the sun was like a personal balm, the ocean breeze a caress. She ate two of the pineapple halves and three bananas. "I've always liked fruit," she explained to Mary as the other woman watched her, eyebrows raised.

"I've heard of the power of suggestion but this is ridiculous. Just because I've told you you could be pregnant does not mean that you immediately have to develop cravings."

"I like fruit." Derry glared at her, reaching for an apple, glad that the queasiness of earlier was gone.

Before Mary left that day she invited Aaron and Derry to dinner at her home in St. George's. "It isn't like Windrift, but we like it very much."

"We would be delighted to come to dinner on Friday. That's a good day for us because Aaron always tries to be home on the weekends."

"Are you going to tell him tonight that you're pregnant?" Mary asked, telling the children to strap on their seat belts as they prepared to leave for home.

"Ah . . . Mary, could you not say anything to anyone for awhile?" Derry asked, feeling the blood rise in her face as Mary looked at her and nodded. "It's just that I'd like to get used to the idea myself first. Oh, and check with a doctor."

That evening when Aaron called from St. Thomas and said that he had reached a snag and wouldn't be home until Friday, she felt relief and disappointment all at once. "Derry? Derry are you there? Is something wrong? Derry, answer me." He growled the last words.

"No. Nothing is wrong. I'm trying to talk to you. We must have a poor connection. I hope you unravel the snafu."

"Is your tummy upset from the water? Have you been regular?"

Derry had to cover her mouth with her hand to keep from both laughing and crying. "I'm fine," she managed to say. "Goodbye, Aaron. I'll see you on Friday." She put down the phone with a muted click, staring at it for long moments, then turned to walk out onto the lanai. She heard voices and laughter come around the house and pushed herself back into the shadows. It was Jim and Barrows and from the remarks they made back and forth, it was clear they were going into Hamilton for a little night life. Bermuda had night life, Derry mused to herself as she heard the car drive away, a smile lifting her lips as she thought of the two eager men who would be seeking it out with a vengeance.

She walked back into the lounge area, fingering the slip of paper that Mary had given her with the address and phone number of the physician that she had used when the twins were born. "Henry Lawrence, M.D." Derry stared at the written name. What would he tell her? She tried to smother her excitement as she mounted the curving stairway to the bedroom she shared with Aaron. Aaron! What would he think? She couldn't even come up with a vague surmise. Her mind was blank.

She thought she would toss and turn but after a cooling shower, she slipped between the sheets, closed her eyes and was gone.

The next day, after she and Sara had walked Kim and Lee to the bus and returned to the house in slow motion with Tom E. Cat jumping around them and at every flying thing, she resolved to call Dr. Lawrence and make an appointment.

It surprised Derry when the nurse said that the doctor would see her on Friday morning. She held her breath for a moment trying to decide if Aaron might come back to Bermuda early in the day. "All right. Ten-thirty is fine. I'll be there."

Derry took the children to the beach by herself when Lee and Kim returned from school because Telford had taken time to do some errands. For some reason Kim was querulous. She quarreled with Lee and snapped at Sara, whose face trembled as she stumbled toward Derry.

"Come here, Kim." She called to the child after Sara was soothed and returned to Lee's side. "Sit down next to me in the shade for a while." She patted the blanket next to her.

For long moments they sat there staring out at the wave-flecked turquoise expanse.

"Derry, am I fat? Am I stupid? Cynthia Bills said that I'm a fat, stupid Yankee. Am I?"

"No, you are not. You are Kimberley Lathrop, whose Da has told her many times that she is his beautiful girl. Is Cynthia smarter than Da?"

Kim stared up at her, then a slow smile creased

the deepening tan of her face. "Nobody is smarter than Da."

"That's what I think, too," Derry said in measured tones, hating herself for believing the words. "So I'm glad that you agree with me that Cynthia couldn't be very smart if she doesn't know what Da knows."

Kim's head bobbed up and down, her dimples very evident. She stood, wiping sand from her thigh. "I guess I better tell Sara that I'll help her build a sand castle." She looked sideways at Derry. "Maybe I should help Lee too."

"That's a good idea." Derry watched the little girl skip toward the others and felt a momentary pang because there would be times when Kim would suffer similar pain, perhaps more intense. Would she always come and tell her mother? Derry felt the crease between her eyes. How many times had Lee suffered indignities and not said anything? She leaned against the back of the beach chair and watched the children. Being a parent was a hard job. Why do I have the urge to wrap them in cotton batten and never let hurt touch them again? Are all parents this way? Derry sighed.

By the time she convinced them it was time to go up for dinner she was as tired as Sara. She barely kept her eyes open while she supervised the girls' baths.

"Mrs. Lathrop, please. I'll take care of the children. Why don't you kiss them good night, and I'll do the rest."

Derry tried to smile at the woman and found herself smothering a yawn instead. She nodded, made her rounds with the kisses and the prayers and the hugs and left for her own suite of rooms on the other side of the house. Not for the first time, she blessed Aaron's insistence on a nanny.

Having someone stay in the children's wing each night was such a comfort to her.

After assuring herself that Tom E. was in his bed in the small pantry close to Lazslo's quarters, Derry mounted the stairs for the last time that day.

She surfaced from sleep like she had struggled from under an avalanche of cotton balls. " 'Lo." She licked her dry lips as she answered the phone.

"Darling, did I wake you? It's only nine-thirty. What are you doing in bed so early? Are you ill? Derry, tell me. What is it?"

"Nothing. I spent too much time in the sun and I'm tired."

"Oh? Are the kids fine? I miss them too."

"Uh? Yes. The children are marvelous." Derry felt the heat rising in her face as she thought of her appointment with Dr. Lawrence the next day and the panic rising in her at the idea of telling Aaron. She gulped in relief as she thought it wouldn't be proper to discuss her news with Aaron on the phone.

"What is it, Derry?" Aaron's voice seemed to drop a decibel as the hunter stalked his quarry.

"Nothing." Her mind balked and turned blank at the unnerving suspicion that he might be reading her mind long distance. "This call must be expensive."

"Derry."

"Aaron, I really must get back to sleep. I'm so tired."

"All right." His words sounded as if they were being driven into a steel plate. "I'll see you tomorrow afternoon."

Derry looked at the phone receiver in her hand, the buzz telling her the connection was broken. "Don't hurry," she whispered through plastic lips.

She knew that she would toss and turn after that conversation with Aaron. She forgot the power of the sun and ocean breeze. She nodded off into deep sleep still convinced that she wouldn't be able to close her eyes.

The next day, Kim and Lee went off to school at a run down the drive, Derry following more slowly with Sara in tow. Sara had a runny nose, which Telford assured her was just an adjunct of too much sun the day before. Derry felt protective with a pinch of guilt because she had allowed the baby to catch cold. She smiled at Telford and agreed with her that the sniffles was nothing. That didn't chase the guilt away, though. Halfway down the drive she lifted the baby into her arms, cuddling and murmuring to her as they followed the more exuberant Kim and Lee.

Before Lee enetered the bus after his sister, he ran back to Derry's side. "Kim feels better today. I can tell."

Derry swallowed at the sensitivity of the quiet boy, a sting of pride in her eyes that this was her son.

For the rest of the morning Sara was fractious and didn't want Derry to leave her. It was a relief when the baby fell asleep and Derry could ready herself for her appointment with Dr. Lawrence.

When Derry went out for the car, Lazslo informed her that Jim and Barrow had taken the two cars, one to pick up supplies for the house and the other to leave the car at the airport for Aaron. Derry realized there wasn't a car available to her. She took a deep breath and asked Lazslo for the keys to Jim's moped. "Don't worry, I have been practicing on the side roads and I'm much more at ease on the bike."

She assured Lazslo that she didn't have far to travel. She neglected to inform him that Dr. Lawrence's office was on the busy road to Hamilton.

Derry was proud of the way she handled the bike, even when a bus honked as it passed her, she had the nerve to wave the driver on. She reached the office without incident, pleased with herself.

Much to her surprise she was ushered into the doctor's office at once. Even more surprising was the youth of Dr. Lawrence. Derry figured that he couldn't have been much older than Aaron. His congenial competency made the rather long examination bearable. When he told her to dress and meet him in his office and the nurse helped to lift her to sitting position on the examining table, Derry could hardly move for the shaking in her limbs.

"Is this your first, dear?" The plump lady with the salt-and-pepper bun and the heavily starched uniform asked her in a kindly way. She helped zip Derry's skirt and handed her purse to her.

"In a way." Derry smiled in a wobbly fashion at the woman. Before she could ask more, Derry left the examining room and went down the short corridor to the doctor's office. She seated herself in front of his desk, not saying anything as the doctor kept writing in a folder that Derry assumed was hers.

He looked up and smiled. "You're in good shape, Mrs. Lathrop. Perhaps you could use a bit more weight and your blood could be somewhat better, but all in all you are about two months pregnant and doing well."

"That far along?" Derry stared at him, her calculations telling her that she must have conceived just days after they married.

Dr. Lawrence's eyebrows arched. "Yes, that far. Is something wrong?"

Derry shook her head slowly. She thanked the doctor, promising him that she would exercise but not overdo, that she would get plenty of fresh air. She rose to leave with the air of a somnambulist. She mumbled her goodbyes to the doctor, clutched her vitamin prescription in her hand and walked through the reception room, looking neither left nor right.

She started to sing as she maneuvered the moped back along the way to Windrift. She noticed that passing motorists looked at her, but she paid no attention. She waved to a busload of people, her slightly off-key alto voice belting out the lyrics to "It's a Most Unusual Day". Several persons out in their yards waved to her, and a lovely man, who owned a miniature horse called "Tommy" and an assortment of cockatiels in all colors, shouted "Hallo."

Derry waved at everyone, and when she reached the entrance to Windrift she whirled into the driveway with a flourish, her song cut off in mid note as she saw the Ferrari coming at her, a grimfaced Aaron at the wheel. She stopped with what she thought was admirable panache, even though it didn't seem to her that the alighting Aaron shared her enthusiasm.

"Don't you bloody well ever listen when I speak to you?" he snarled, coming toward her and lifting her from the bike. His mouth met hers, his tongue gently thrusting into her own. "How the hell do I get you to behave?" he muttered into her hair, his arm not releasing her.

"I listen," Derry said in a squeaky voice.

"If I wasn't so damned upset by the phone message Lazslo gave me, I'd really chew your ear off, wife." His tongue marked a passage up her neck.

"What message?" Derry closed her eyes in delight as Aaron nibbled at her neck.

"My family is coming to Bermuda to visit."

Derry groaned. "Oh, Lord, how horrible!"

Aaron's laugh sounded harsh to her ears.

Eight

Derry knew that if she had had a month to prepare for the visit instead of six days it would not
have been enough. She dreaded the arrival of Aaron's mother and father, Aunt Sylvie, Cousin Donald, Cousin Irene, and whoever else would tag
along. The Lathrop family traveled as an en-
tourage—never singly. They crossed worlds with
cat carriers and one thousand dollars worth of pet
food guaranteed to soothe Kitty's tum tum. Derry's eyes crossed in pain as she remembered the
time that Aunt Sylvie had brought her pug dog to
their apartment. Derry had felt sorry for the obese
thing that seemed to have no legs or eyes. She felt
sorry for it until it heaved its dinner onto the rug
in front of the fireplace, and Aunt Sylvie had
scolded Derry for having had such rich food around
as to make Popo ill. Popo had eaten Aunt Sylvie's
homemade eclair from her plate as Aaron's rela-
tive had been discoursing on the wisdom of people marrying within their own class. Since Popo

had insisted on sitting on Aunt Sylvie's lap during the meal, he had had perfect access to the dessert. Aaron, who had been at a business dinner that evening, had not been able to understand Derry's semi-hysterics when she had described the incident to him later in the evening. When he had begun to laugh, Derry had been furious with him and they had quarreled.

Derry remembered all these things. And because of the family's imminent arrival, she hadn't given Aaron her big news.

She checked guest quarters with Lazslo the morning of the Lathrops' arrival. "You're right, of course, Lazslo. The rooms are just fine. I—I think that Mr. Lathrop's parents will like the Rose Room and Mrs. Kent will enjoy the view of the garden." Derry said not believing for a moment that Aunt Sylvie would be satisfied with anything. She could feel her lips thinning against her teeth. If the old harridan says anything nasty to the children, she'll deal with me, Derry thought, balling her hands into fists. "What did you say, Lazslo? Oh no. Nothing is wrong." She looked around at the tall Bermudian, unflexing her fingers. "And the menus are in order . . . all those things I wanted ordered?"

"Yes ma'am. Cook knows not to serve Mr. Lathrop shellfish and there are *brioches* for Mrs. Kent." His wooden visage relaxed for a moment. "Trust me, ma'am. I know the two ladies . . . er, well."

Derry sighed, then looked at her watch. "Oh, Lord, look at the time. Mr. Lathrop will have picked them up at the airport by now. I have to change. Lazslo . . ." Derry hotfooted it from the room, her voice streaming behind her. ". . . make sure the drinks cart is on the terrace. And don't forget cheese and crackers . . ." Derry threw her clothes on, smearing her lip gloss twice. By the time she was in the halter dress, her hands were perspiring and she could feel a beading of moisture on her upper lip.

She was pressing cold cloths onto her wrists when Telford brought the children to her room.

"The car is coming up the drive, Mrs. Lathrop," she informed Derry, the sparkle in her eye telling her she understood.

Derry lifted Sara, giving her a cuddle. She looked down at Kim and Lee, nodding. "Well, if they don't like us, they can go plumb to h—" Derry saw Lee's alert look. "—plumb to Barbados." She felt the smile fold like an accordion on her face as she followed the children down the wide sweep of stairs just as the hall door was opened by Lazslo. "Charge," Derry whispered.

It wasn't until she was on the last step that she noticed that Tom E. Cat was standing facing a corner of the hall, hackles raised, hissing. "What in . . ." Derry began, looking in horrified fascination as whatever Tom E. had cornered made a break for it right across the hall in front of the opening door.

"Tom is chasing the lizard again, Lee." Kim belled, goggle-eyed as the lizard ran between the legs of the woman entering the house.

"Stop that, Tom." Lee called as the shrieking began. "That's my lizard, Abraham."

"Abraham." Derry repeated weakly, closing her eyes for a moment as she heard Aaron swear, then shout.

"Lazslo, grab my aunt. That damned cat tripped her. Mother, just calm yourself. Father, take her arm. What the bleeding hell is going on here?"

"Is Aaron swearing, Pendleton?" Aaron's mother moaned.

"Can't say. In this crazy house there looks to be a

great deal to swear about." His father harumphed, shushing his keening wife.

"Throw cold water onto her, Pendleton." Aunt Sylvie spat the words into the hassle, then steamed through the front door like Old Ironsides in full sail. "Ah, there you are, Derry. How are you, girl? a bit thin, I should say. Why you girls want to look like licorice whips, I'll never know! Whose fool cat was that? The thing should be drowned. It's a nuisance."

The door was swept wide and the others spilled into the hall, a grim-faced Aaron bringing up the rear with Lazslo and Barrow. "Dammit. Where is that Jim when you need him?" Aaron gnashed his teeth.

"No." Kim shouted, standing in front of Derry. Lee came up next to her. "No, you won't drown our cat. I won't let you."

Aaron stared at the children, openmouthed.

Aunt Sylvie's nostrils flared and she inhaled deeply.

Before the woman could speak Derry stepped around the two children, still holding Sara in her arms. "No, of course no one is going to drown Tom E., but I think you should tell Aunt Sylvie that you are sorry for shouting, don't you?" Derry spoke in quiet tones, aware of the surcease of noise around her. She kept her eyes on Kim all the while.

Kim swallowed. "I didn't mean to shout. Sorry."

Derry smiled at the child as Aaron came forward and swept Kim into his arms and gestured Lee forward. "Of course you didn't mean to shout. You're a good girl. I know that." His look brought a smile to the child's face. Then he looked at the lizard Lee was sheltering with his body while he shooed Tom E. Aaron put Kim down on her feet. "Take Tom to the kitchen, Kim, until Lee can take care of . . . Abraham." Aaron turned to look at Derry, a smile on his face. "When did he adopt the lizard?"

"A few days ago." Derry shrugged, cuddling the wide-eyed Sara who in turn hugged her "huggy banky." "I hadn't realized he had named it." Derry stepped forward, watching Aaron's mother who was taking deep breaths and muttering about animals being kept outside. "How are you, Mrs. Lathrop? Mr. Lathrop?"

"Well, Derry, it seems you are married to my son once more." Mrs. Lathrop took a deep breath and was about to continue when Lazslo stepped forward and told her that there was tea in the lounge, if she would just follow him.

Derry stayed in the hall for long moments, her eyes closed, blessing the Bermudian who had fobbed off her mother in law for a few moments and wondering how long she could take the company of Aaron's family.

"Open your eyes and stop building mountains. It won't be bad. I won't let it be." Aaron pulled her close to his side, pressing his mouth to her hair. He smiled when Sara held out her arms to him, reaching for the child at once. "Come along, Derry. I want to introduce the children to Mother and Father."

"Why? So they can boil *all* of us in oil instead of just me?" she muttered to his back, her steps dragging as she followed him into the lounge.

The children were duly introduced to the family. Derry held her breath until Telford came for the children and took them from the room.

Cousin Donald's thin face quivered in distaste. His horn-rimmed glasses looked opaque in the sunlight streaming from the open french doors. "My God, Aaron, we've never had orientals in our fam . . ." Cousin Donald's voice faded when Aaron surged to his feet, his teeth bared. "What I mean is . . . ah . . . it is certainly a unique experience in the Lathrop family."

Aaron opened his mouth, but Derry spoke first after hastily clearing her throat. "That's all right, Donald, old boy. When I first met you I thought you were the comic relief in the Lathrop family. Which proves that you can get used to anything."

"See here—" Donald began.

"Pendleton, is Derry being unkind to Donald?" Mrs. Lathrop asked.

"Now listen—" Cousin Irene seemed to swell.

Aaron guffawed, making all heads turn his way. The silence stretched as Aaron lifted his glass and toasted his wife.

"Picked up a little starch, hasn't she?" Aunt Sylvie seemed to expel the words directly from her adenoids. "I shall pour the tea, Lazslo."

"No, Lazslo, I shall do it," Derry said mildly, her heart pumping out of rhythm. She sat down on the blue settee, inclining her head to the Bermudian who at once set the silver tray embossed with Sir Rupert's crest in front of her, the trays of cakes and dainties on either side of the tea tray. "Do you still take lemon, Sylvie?" Derry stared at the woman blandly, aware that her raised eyebrows were because Derry had not tacked "Aunt" in front of her name. "Or would you prefer cream and sugar?"

"Plain." Her perfect maquillage seemed to crack a little as she took the cup from Derry's hand.

Derry passed a cup to each person, inquiring first about his taste.

"She might have remembered that I take cream and sugar, Pendleton." Aaron's mother sighed, stirring once to right, twice to left.

"Why?" Derry smiled. "Your taste might have changed. It happens."

"Not to me." Mrs. Lathrop blinked several times and pursed her lips.

"Take a damper, Adelia," Mr. Lathrop said as he received his cup from Derry, nodding once when she held the cream pitcher over his cup. He coughed. "Like those kids, Derry. Good bottom. Aaron always had good bottom despite my wife and sister."

"Pendleton," Adelia wailed.

"You're an ass, Pendleton," Sylvie hissed, making Adelia ask what the world was coming to.

"I think"—Cousin Donald rose to his feet, taking a sip of his tea—"that Derry should be grateful to live in this fine old home." He sniffed. "I hope my accomodations will be as comfortable this time as they have been previously." He shot an owlish look at Derry, standing very close to Aunt Adelia so that he barely noticed Aaron clenching and unclenching his hands.

Derry looked up at Cousin Donald with a smile. "Why don't you get a room at the Loew's Bermuda Beach? It isn't far and then you can be absolutely sure of your *accomodations*." Derry looked down into her teacup as the snorts, "now listen"s, and "well I never"s swelled and ebbed around her.

"Well, Aaron, what do you say to that?" Aunt Sylvie sounded out each word.

"I disagree with Derry. I think Donald would prefer the Princess. It's in Hamilton, closer to the tourist traps." Aaron handed his cup to Derry to be refilled.

Again the myriad mutters rose in the room.

"So that's the way the wind blows does it?" Aunt Sylvie's voice was quite mild, her mink brown eyes snapping in instant comprehension.

Irene licked her lips, stared at her mother for a moment, looked at her brother, and opened her mouth.

"Drop it, Irene." Aaron said gently, his words falling among the assembly like cotton rockets.

"So, Aaron," Aunt Sylvie exhaled through her nose, "you are happy with these children?"

Again Derry spoke before Aaron could answer. "We are no different than any other parents. Some days it is easier to love our children than others, but even when we must struggle to love them they are unquestionably our children."

"Pendleton, has Derry always interrupted Aaron this way?" Mrs. Lathrop asked, her voice rising in plaintive cadence.

"Girl's got good bottom too." Aaron's father answered, surprise in his voice.

"Madame." Lazslo spoke in his most freezing British accent. "The rooms are ready for your guests. Would you like it if I show them up?" Since Lazslo had never taken on the job of dictating when guests should be taken to their rooms, there were several surprised faces turned his way.

"Yes, thank you, Lazslo, that will be fine," Aaron answered for a bemused Derry.

"Formed an army, have you, Derry?" Aunt Sylvie surged to her feet, the delicate Irish damask napkin balled in her fist. She led the way out of the lounge. "I assume that dinner is at eight?"

"Seven, madame. The children enjoy an after dinner chat with their parents." Lazslo announced in lofty tones, looking over the heads of the people turned his way.

"But I told him we would move up the dinner hour." Derry mumbled as Aaron took her arm and led her up the stairway to their suite of rooms, situated on the family side of the house.

Aaron chuckled as he shepherded her through the door of their sitting room and closed it behind him. "Lazslo has a very profound understanding about the pecking order at Windrift. Guests are treated with the utmost courtesy, but they must never be allowed to interfere with the family."

"Oh, I see." Derry turned to face him, her pulse speeding up as she watched Aaron cast aside the shirt he was wearing, then move toward her in fluid fashion. "Trip successful?" Derry asked, a catch in her voice.

"Very." Aaron bent over her, his hands not touching her, his lips brushing back and forth on hers. His teeth nipped at her bottom lip, making her mouth open even more.

"Good to discuss your day." Derry swallowed, trying hard to keep her eyes open, but not succeeding.

"I'll tell all." Aaron muttered, his hands making short work of the buttons on her sheer cotton dress. "You look gorgeous in this blue thing. I could see the narrow space between your thighs while we were downstairs. I didn't like the idea of Donald or my father seeing the same thing." He frowned down at her body. "You didn't wear a bra."

"It has a lining in the top." Derry felt as though her tongue had doubled in size. Her words had a fuzzy sound as she tried to push them past her lips.

"You don't need a bra." Aaron leaned down his tongue licking at the beading of moisture between her breasts. "You have lovely, firm breasts." His hand kneaded the flesh under his hand with loving concentration, a puzzling crease to his lazy smile. "I think Bermuda is good for you, darling. Your breasts are getting fuller, even though you don't seem to have gained weight elsewhere." The frown deepened again. "You should gain weight."

"Chances are I will." Derry leaned back from him. "That's what I'd like to talk to you about . . . one of the things anyway." Derry groaned as Aaron continued to disrobe her, part of her mind taking note of the cavalier treatment he afforded her clothes.

"You want to talk about weight gain? Now? Hell, Derry, your timing is the bottom of quick-sand . . . nowhere," Aaron muttered, his words more slurred.

"But—"

"Derry, we'll talk later, all night, whenever you wish, but not now." Aaron swept her high in his arms, his eyes glittering as he took in her naked body, blood rising in his face. "I may not even let you go down for dinner."

"Aaron." Derry was half amused, half alarmed. Then as he lowered her to the bed and followed her down she forgot everything but that Aaron wanted her, and she wanted Aaron. How she loved that hard-muscled body, which covered hers like a pulsing blanket.

They had made love many times in their years together, and Derry had always considered it exciting and good, but today it had a subtle difference, a nuance that she couldn't quite name. The explosions were there, but they were serene eruptions, dynamite calm, soothing hurricanes. For the first time in their lovemaking, Derry sensed an elusive control coming from Aaron to her. With a delicate sweep, Derry let her hands rove his body, the hardening response an erotic trigger to her own feelings. As her hands kneaded his lower body, clutching the muscular buttocks, his gasp of pleasure pleasured her.

Their foreplay increased in intensity as though each was determined that the other have greater joy.

When his mouth made a foray down her body, Derry was sure that her blood would burst through her veins. They climbed higher, to the peak of feeling. Whirling in slow, sensuous circles into the vortex, Derry knew without a shadow of doubt that there was no one else for her on this planet, that Aaron was her own, one true love. The happy despair she felt only increased her pulsating desire. "Aaron."

"Yes, darling." He groaned, ministering to her body with shaking lips.

"I'm—I'm . . ." Her head thrashed on the pillow as Aaron's power over her reasserted itself, his hand going on whirling motions on her abdomen. "I'm drowning."

"Drown in me, love. Disappear in me."

"Aaron." Derry didn't recognize the raspy voice as her own as she felt his mouth at her thighs.

Derry felt the waves of need wash over her, her want for Aaron like a tidal wave that brooked no resistance. She tugged at the hair on his head to pull him up her body.

"Yes, love, I know. I'm coming to you. Be patient." He laughed thickly.

"No," Derry gasped, her body expanding with desire, lungs and heart swelling with pressure. "I don't want to be patient."

As his body closed over hers, the tip of his tongue prodded into the warmth of her mouth. "You've put a torch to me, wife of mine." Aaron's guttural murmur penetrated the golden haze surrounding them. "You've burned me to a cinder."

"Aaron," she cried. Her voice was convulsing with a cosmic energy that seared through her and into Aaron. Her body tightened around him as she felt his spasmodic response.

"Derry . . . Derry, darling."

The fragrance of the early Bermuda evening was balmy in the room, the perfume of hibiscus melding with the steamy aura of their passion.

Derry breathed deeply, her arms still around Aaron as she drifted into sleep.

She heard the muffled guns being fired at Fort St. Catherine's and decided that she must open her eyes.

"Who the hell's at the door?" Aaron muttered into her neck.

"Oh. I thought they were firing the cannons."

"What?" Aaron yawned hugely, kissed her hard on the mouth, and rose from the bed. "Who is it? Is something wrong?"

"It's Sylvie, Aaron. Let me in."

Derry pulled the covers to her chin. Aaron caught the movement and gave her a hard grin, throwing the terry coverup around his waist.

He opened the door but barricaded the opening with his body. "What is it, Sylvie?"

"Shouldn't you invite me in?"

"No," Aaron answered, his forward stance uncompromising.

"When did you get so discourteous, Aaron?"

"When people started coming to my bedroom uninvited. You shouldn't expect a glad hand, Sylvie." His voice held a hard mockery, his rigid shoulders telling Derry more than anything that he was very irritated. His Bostonian accent was getting stronger.

"Very well." Sylvie sniffed. "I only wanted to tell you that we saw Ern Griswold in Cap d'Antibes. He said he would follow us out here. I insisted that he visit us. I know how close you two were at Harvard."

Derry sat bolt upright in bed when Aaron slammed the door hard enough to make the sound reverberate like a gong. "You had better open the door and . . ." Derry's voice trailed when she saw the green lava look to his eyes, his teeth bared like a wolf on the attack.

"I damn well won't open that door," he snarled, then whirled from her to the bathroom, again slamming the door, making Derry jump.

"Well, damn you to hell, Mr. Aaron Lathrop. Just what gives you the right to spew like a volcano over everyone?" Derry threw back the covers and hopped to the floor in a fighter's stance facing the bathroom. "You . . . you chameleon, you." She shouted this last then whirled toward the other bathroom still muttering imprecations. "Do you know something, Mr. Bad Tempered Lathrop?" She snarled, turning the taps viciously in the round tub. "I never used to swear at all until I was married to you." She glared at the Joy essence container she was pouring into the tub.

She sank down into the fragrant depths, sighing.

She shot bolt upright at the sound of banging on the door.

"Derry, you don't have time for a bath. Shower. Ern Griswold will be here for dinner, so I'm informed," Aaron yelled through the door.

"Turn blue," Derry muttered, sinking lower in the water, her fond feelings for him evaporating in his angry tone.

"Derry. Derry. Damn you, answer me. I'll break the damn door."

"Stop swearing. I'll be out when I'm through."

"Derry." Aaron threatened her.

"Go away."

For long moments Derry thought he might, indeed, smash the door. Then she heard him mumble something and leave.

She had every intention of hurrying, but the combination of hot water and upset with Aaron had a punchy effect on her metabolism. She napped again. When she awakened, the water was considerably cooler.

It wasn't until she left the bathroom, makeup

applied, dressed in apricot-colored undies, that she realized that it was already forty-five minutes past the time that the cocktail hour was scheduled to start. She dressed hurriedly, moaning in despair when she looked into the mirror. What devil had made her don the punjabis? Her in-laws would be horrified, Sylvie contemptuous and sarcastic, Donald . . . Oh, who cared what he thought? Derry asked herself swallowing. It was too late to change from the deep-rose-colored tightly cuffed chiffon pants, which showed a great deal of leg through the sheer silkiness. She tugged at the tunic, which almost reached her knees. Surely that would cover her. Not bloody likely, she wailed in silence as she studied the slits that opened up both sides of the tunic. The long sleeves were cuffed in the same fashion as the pants, and her skin showed like pink pearl through the iridescent silk. The neckline of the tunic was boat-shaped, so that the straight-falling garment barely clung to the tips of her shoulders. With it she wore deep rose *peau de soie* heelless sandals. Her jewelry was a pink sapphire ring with matching drop earrings. She had pulled her hair into a chignon at the base of her neck, pierced through with two pink bone picks.

The outfit had been sent to her by Dev and Sandy for her birthday during her first marriage to Aaron, but she had never worn it. She had packed it with her things when she had intended to marry Gerard. She had no idea why she had pulled it from the closet today and had had the maid air the garment and press it.

She twisted this way and that. Her eye caught the time on the bedside clock. Gasping, she forgot all about her ambivalent feelings concerning the punjabis and fled from the room, sped down the hall, and took the steps two at a time. The chil-

dren would be in the lounge with the guests.
Derry groaned. Maybe they had already been sent
to their rooms. She gritted her teeth, coming to a
skidding halt in front of the closed lounge doors.
She would get the children back. They were used
to a long relaxing time with their parents before
bed.

She thrust open the double doors, geared for
battle, unaware that the coin-sized spots of color
high on her cheekbones gave her an exotic look,
her uplifted chin a regal air, her heaving bosom a
very sexy picture. She paused in the doorway as
heads turned toward her.

"There's Derry," Kim caroled.

Lee smiled.

Sara pushed against Aaron's shoulder to get
down, chanting "Dawy, Dawy, Dawy."

Aaron and Ern Griswold approached right on
the heels of the children. Ern was just a shade
ahead of Aaron. Derry wondered about her husband's grim look for just a moment when Ern,
who was almost as large as Aaron, swung her into
his arms.

"Derry, darling, you're beautiful. Why the hell
did you have to marry the beast again when you
could have married me, Prince Charming."

Derry laughed, relaxing a bit. "Ern, you are still
a fool. It is so good to see you." She clasped his
arms and smiled up at him, stunned when he
bent and placed a hard kiss on her mouth.

"Ummm, you taste good, lady." Ern smiled down
at her.

Before she could say anything, she felt herself
lifted away from Ern, Aaron barely setting her
down on the floor as he enfolded her close to him.
"Aaron! Aaron, for heaven's sake, my tunic . . .
It's crept up. Put me down," she said in a low,
angry voice.

Aaron let her feet touch the floor but didn't release her, even when she struggled to straighten her clothing.

"Really, Derry you might try to be on time," Mother Lathrop whined. "Pendleton is thirsty."

"Am not. Helped myself to a drink."

Derry smiled at her father-in-law gratefully. When he winked and saluted her with his glass she was taken aback. "I'm sorry. I lost track of time." She saw Kim reach for one of the canapes, the crystal dish of macadamia nuts rocking. Then, even as Derry watched, the little girl turned, the bow on the back of her dress catching a Waterford plate of French craquelins. The crackers flew farther than the dish.

When Lee and Derry made a dive for the dish they nearly collided. Neither saved the dish, which probably wouldn't have broken if it had landed on the Oriental rug without hitting the leg of the teakwood table.

"Oh dear! Those children!" Mother Lathrop rolled back her eyes. "That Waterford has been in the family for years."

"God, can't you control them, Aaron?" Sylvie's lips tightened, her eyebrows arching as she stared at the saucer-eyed Kim, one pebble-sized tear trickling from each eye.

"Children should be seen and not heard," Irene opined, as though it were an original thought. She folded the hem of her jonquil-colored chiffon dress close to her body as though she might be tainted.

Ern strode across the room as Aaron whirled from the bar. He scooped Kim high into his arms and patted Lee, whose jaw and body were thrusted toward Sylvie and Irene, on the head. "Did I ever tell you about the time I threw a rock through the window of my home and shattered my grandfather's display case of Sevres china?"

Sara toddled over to Ern, and the other two shook their heads, distracted from the fuming adults around them.

"Don't you tell me where my children should or should not be," Aaron roared, his anger puzzling Derry. She watched his head swivel from Ern and the children to Sylvie, Donald, and Irene, who were clustered near the fireplace.

"Pendleton." Mother Lathrop clutched at her forehead. "Do I hear Aaron shouting? I shall get one of my headaches."

"Go ahead," Pendleton mumbled, watching his son through narrowed eyes.

"And then I shall feel queasy all evening. Do tell Aaron to take the children away . . . at least until they are more civilized."

"Bushwaugh," he answered, not taking his eyes from Aaron, who was standing in the corner, not quite pawing the ground, snorting, and grinding his teeth.

"This is my home, and these are my children. And tonight they will be dining with us."

"We ate, Da." Kim smiled at her father from Ern's shoulder. Sara and Lee nodded.

Derry moved to Ern's side and reached up for Kim. Ern put his hand on Derry's waist as he released Kim to her with the other arm.

"And you take your bloody hand off my wife or I'll break your arm."

Derry could barely hear the feeble moans of her mother-in-law, the disgusted sniffs of Irene and Sylvie, the cracked voice of Donald saying "Lord." She did hear her father in law mutter "Charge."

Nine

Windrift was like a tomb. The balmy Bermuda breezes entered the house with weird loudness. It was as though no one lived there.

Derry shook her head, trying to still the shiver that assailed her as she thought of the last two days and Aaron's cold-as-the-Arctic attitude. It amazed her that he hadn't driven his family and Ern Griswold away from Windrift. Instead he had informed her in cast iron words that his sisters and their families would be joining the rest of the Lathrop clan. Derry groaned as she climbed the last stretch of driveway from the road, holding Sara's pudgy hand in hers. At least Lee and Kim had school as an escape.

"Good morning, Derry." Mr. Lathrop stepped from behind an hibiscus bush, holding out a blossom to the gleeful Sara. "And how is Grandpa's big girl this morning?" A smile creased his face, making Derry realize how much Aaron looked like his father.

"Good." Sara held up her arms. "Up."

Pendleton Lathrop gulped, then scooped the child into his arms, cuddling her close, chuckling when she patted him on the cheek. "They are such beautiful children, Derry. When I see Lee watching over that lizard Abraham, it reminds me of his father when he was a boy. Aaron always brought everything home."

Derry smiled at her father-in-law when he insisted on carrying the chubby youngster with her head on his shoulder.

"Are you sure she isn't too heavy?" Derry made a halfhearted protest, realizing in the last few days that Grandpa Lathrop was, indeed, falling in love with his grandchildren, and he sought their company at every turn. It had been he who had insisted that the children continue to take their meals with the adults and had horrified his wife by suggesting that they might eat even earlier so that the children wouldn't be too tired at the table.

Derry had quashed that, knowing that the children would be far more relaxed eating by themselves with just Telford, Aaron, and herself in attendance. Of course Grandpa Lathrop joined them.

"Gappa." Sara sighed, the black curtain of her hair spread on his shoulder.

Pendleton Lathrop sighed, too. "I wish I could live here on Bermuda, Derry, just so that I could be close to the children, but"—he gave her an elfin grin—"I feel that it's my duty as a Lathrop to keep that devil's brood away from you and Aaron as much as possible."

Derry stared at him.

"Oh yes." He nodded, giving the baby a soft kiss on the cheek. "I saw the havoc the family wreaked on your marriage the first time around." His face took on a grim look. "And I regret very much my part in it."

Derry put her hand on his arm. "Don't say that. A marriage falls apart because of the two people involved. No one else."

"Derry, my child, what you say is mostly true, but there can be Chinese water torture in marriage too. I watched my wife and my sister pull down the hurricane on your head when Aaron wasn't around. I watched them feed Aaron's jealousy of you—"

"Aaron isn't jealous," Derry whispered dryly.

"My dear child!" He smiled at her as he paused on the lanai to look around him as though he sought privacy, then settled both himself and Sara on a bamboo loveseat. The baby was content to hug her blanket and stay on her grandpa's warm lap. "You were and are the greatest thing to come into Aaron's love starved life, and if I had had the courage I would have told you that before instead of letting my family drive an almost irreparable wedge between you." He patted the baby's head absently, his jaw hardening. "When I saw how gleeful Sylvie and my wife were at your divorce I was deeply ashamed, and when I saw how angered they were when you remarried, I determined that I wouldn't let them separate you again."

Derry sighed, feeling a strange weightlessness. "Do you know, Mr. Lathrop—"

"Please call me Pen, my dear."

"Pen. Well, I just don't think they have the power to do that anymore." Derry nodded once in a firm way. "I didn't know it before you arrived here this time, but I know it now." She shrugged, reaching from her chair to the settee and letting her hand fall onto his arm. "It's as though all the things that they tried to do seem ludicrous now. I guess I had some growing up to do." She smiled at the sleepy child cuddled close to her grandfather. "Perhaps the children pulled me outside myself so that I could get a close look at the self-conscious and *very* young woman who married Aaron the first time."

"You love him, don't you?" Pen asked gently.

"Well . . . yes, very much. I always have. Damn the man," she muttered as her father-in-law chuckled.

"Then why haven't you told him that you're going to have a fourth child?" His bland tone disarmed Derry.

"Oh dear, how did you know? I don't know why I haven't told him. Do you think that the rest of them have guessed?" Derry looked down the front of herself.

"That self-engrossed gaggle? Don't be ridiculous."

"Why is she being ridiculous?" Aaron asked from the bottom of the fan-shaped steps leading to the lanai.

"What are you doing home?" Derry rose. "I thought you were going to be in St. Thomas for the day."

"Did you?" Aaron glowered at his father. "I decided that I could do most of this work in my study. I hope I haven't inconvenienced you by my decision." He fired the words like missiles; his chin seemed to push at his skin when he heard his father chuckle.

"I'll take Sara up for her nap." Pen beamed at Derry as he rose to his feet with the child in his arms. "See what I mean?" He shot the words at Derry, winking at her.

"Yes, Pen, I think I'm beginning to," Derry replied, her expression benign.

"What the hell's going on here?" Aaron's body thrust forward like a bull. "Where's he going? What's he mean? Where's Ern? Since when do you call my father Pen?"

Derry lifted a hand to wipe the beading of perspiration on his upper lip, liking the feeling of them being face to face because Aaron was still standing one step down from the terrace and their eyes were level. "Nothing. Upstairs. Nothing. Swimming. Since a few moments ago when he asked me to call him by his name." Derry smiled at the narrow-eyed Aaron, watching his body flex for war.

"Don't get smart with me, Derry. Those one word, serial answers won't put me off." He stepped up to her level, his eyes widening a bit when she didn't retreat. "You think my instincts haven't been honed razor sharp? You think I don't know when my home life is being threatened? I wasn't fooling when I told you that you are married to stay, Derry. You are. Shackled, manacled, tied with wire from head to foot to me for the rest of your life and beyond."

"Makes me feel like Houdini," Derry murmured, her head back as she stared up at him. "Want to go snorkeling?"

"Huh? You and me?" Aaron watched her, eyes narrowed.

"Yes, unless of course you would like to invite—"

"Get your suit. I'll get the equipment." Aaron strode around her, his long legs taking him into the house.

"Yes, sir." Derry saluted, giggling, feeling girlish and carefree. Aaron was jealous, Pen said. He wanted her. He must love her. He would fight for her. She whistled to herself as she ran up the stairs to their wing. *I wonder what he would think if he knew that now I have decided to fight for him, that now I have decided to wipe out any interference in our marriage, that I will blacken the eye of any creature who looks at him . . . and blacken his if he looks back.* Her whistling changed to humming as bloodthirsty pictures unfolded before her eyes of blondes, redheads, and assorted brunettes strewn every which way with bruised eyes. A triumphant Derry, her hands clasped above her head in a victory stance, was poised above the bodies. No more Mister Nice Girl, a cocky Derry thought, pushing back the door to her bedroom and letting it bang against the wall.

She hurried into her bathing suit, clinically studying her figure in the azure blue bikini. "Aaron expects you to wear the one piece, my girl." She preened, poking her tongue at her mirror image. "Hmmmm, your tummy is a little too round for this outfit and your breasts are coming out of the top." She shrugged. "If it falls off, I'll snorkel in the nude." Singing now, she donned a blue towelling robe and pushed her feet into sand clogs.

As she was going down the stairs she met a scowling Jim pacing the front hall. He glared up at her.

"My damn bouillabaisse is going down the tube. Dining on the lanai is out. When the hell are they leaving, Derry? They are driving me and the cook nuts."

Derry stared at Jim. "I want the bouillabaisse *and* dining on the Lanai. If they don't like it, tell them to take a trot into Hamilton for dinner." Derry flipped her head up in the air, not even waiting for Jim's burst of laughter and muffled response that sounded like "Damned if I won't tell them just that."

The beach was deserted . . . or so it seemed to Derry until she saw Aaron surface from the water and swim toward the beach. Before he reached it, Derry heard her name called and turned to see Ern Griswold, a lovely blonde in tow, her streaky hair curling to her shoulders, the pink suit she wore cut to the navel and shearing up her hips to a point almost at her waist. She had almost as much bare body showing as did Derry, and it was a good body, Derry admitted with a grimace.

"Derry, meet Shelly Davis. She's staying at the Princess. We met last night." He grinned at Derry, his eyes running over her like an auctioneer's would.

She sensed Aaron at her back, then felt a wet arm at her waist, the coolness making her shiver.

"Cold, darling?" Aaron folded her closer.

Ern made the introductions.

When Derry saw Shelly arch her body as Aaron took her hand and saw her husband's appreciative smile, she reached up and pinched him hard on the back, her actions hidden from Ern and Shelly. When Aaron sucked in a deep breath it pleased her. His head whipped her way, his eyes narrowed on her, a muscle jumping at the corner of his mouth.

"Mind if Shell and I join you in a little snorkeling?"

Aaron shrugged at Ern. "Not at all."

"Well, since I'm a novice at this perhaps I should go with Aaron." Shelly breathed, breasts pushing against the stretch material. Aaron's mouth quirked in sensual awareness.

"Fine." Ern answered taking Derry's arm. "I'll go with you, pretty lady."

"All right." Derry plotted Aaron's murder as she donned the equipment. She was wondering how to lure a tiger shark into the vicinity as she entered the water next to Ern. In moments she forgot her ire as she entered the silent blue green world. She had the feeling that she could have conversed with the multicolored creatures that floated by her in a graceful underwater ballet. The skeletal coral was a kaleidoscopic pueblo that undersea architects had constructed for her personal pleasure.

As usual she hated to return to her own element. It was Aaron who pulled her out, his hands around her body, dragging her away from the fascination of the ocean. She stumbled out of the water at his side, tugging the mask from her face, feeling a lacing of fatigue.

"Don't you ever learn when to leave it? When you've had enough?" He muttered, putting an arm under her knees and swinging her up into his arms, his growled amusement making Derry's flesh quiver.

When she looked over his shoulder and saw a pouting Shelly following with Ern, it was all she could do not to poke her tongue at the other girl, scream at her "hands off," then laugh in triumph from her perch of safety in Aaron's arms. Safety! Her body jerked. Yes, that was true. She always felt safe when Aaron held her.

"For God's sake, love, lie quiet. You have me staggering all over in this sand." His hard smile delighted her. "Not that I'm complaining at your weight gain. I'm not. I'd just like you not to fight me at every turn."

"All right," Derry said, then let her arms curl around his neck, her mouth at his jawbone.

"Derry, don't." The cords in his neck stiffened under her hands.

"All right." She let her fingers trace the line of resistance in his neck. Lazily absorbed in her task, she didn't notice he had stopped next to their blanket and was looking down at her. The smile she had for him wouldn't be denied. She felt it crack across her face, peeling away the mask of pretense. Win, lose, or draw she was his. Hurt, pain, or the mini death of separation wouldn't change that. Her mouth opened, expelling all the tension she had amassed for so long. Her head lolled back on his shoulder. She inhaled the clean, sweet Bermuda air and with it the resolve to play her cards as they fell. No more trying to beat the system, trying to second guess the stars. No more projection into the future in order to arm herself against hurt. From now on it would be minute by minute, hour by hour, day by day. And this time she knew that she could fight back.

"That face of yours has run the gamut from bliss to mayhem," Aaron pointed out in measured abstraction. "I'm in there somewhere, but where, I wonder."

Derry slid down his body, her fingers pulling at the curling chest hair. "Stick around and find out."

"I intend to. Did you get rapture of the deep out there? You entered the water the tight faced Derry fighting me at every turn and you came out of there like Circe." His rasping chuckle had steel in it.

Ern came up next to Derry taking one of her hands in his and kissing the palm. "Strange, old chum, that you haven't noticed that Derry has always been a Circe."

Derry watched in fascination as blood rose thickly up the column of Aaron's neck and into his face, then receded leaving the bones pushing through the skin in skeletal whiteness. "I notice a lot of things, 'old chum,' some that I think you are unaware of. I'm more than willing to take apart anything or anyone who tries to come at my wife."

Ern looked at him in silky acceptance. "You are welcome to try, old buddy. You had better know that I believe in the adage, winner takes all."

Aaron's body seemed to flex, his mouth curving in a netherworld smile. "Am I to take it that the gauntlet is down?" The words were a sibilant hiss.

Ern inhaled a deep breath, his hands clench-

ing. "Any way you want to take it is fine with me."
His mouth thinned, his eyes never moving from
Aaron's.

Derry cleared her throat.

Neither man looked around at her.

Shelly sauntered up to the two men, ignoring
Derry as though she were invisible, one strap of
her bathing suit down so that her breasts were
almost hanging free at the top. "What will we do
now, Aaron?" Her syrupy voice made Derry grind
her teeth. "I loved being under water with you. It
was so . . . so cosy, if you know what I mean."

Neither man looked at her either.

Derry reached down to pick up one of the bath
sheets belonging to Windrift. "Here. I wouldn't
want you to catch cold." Derry hoped her smile
didn't look like that of the Cheshire Cat in pain.

Shelly blinked at Derry as though she had just
dropped to the sand like some unwelcome genie.
"I'm not cold. Thanks." She turned to the men
again, putting her finger nails, which were lac-
quered a deep plum, on Aaron's bare arm. "I would
like a drink though."

Neither man looked at her.

"I've never felt threatened by you, Aaron. What I
want, I go after . . . no matter who is in the way."
Ern shook free of Shelly when she tried to take
his arm.

"Likewise." Aaron spat the words. He lifted Derry
by one arm, and soon she was trotting at his side
across the beach.

"I do wish you wouldn't make me walk as though
one leg was shorter than the other." Derry panted, only touching the ground every few feet. "My
arm is going numb."

"Oh, I'm sorry." Aaron looked at her in furrowed
abstraction, his Bostonian accent very pronounced.

He watched her mount her moped, his directions precise even though his voice was vague.

Derry wheeled up the grade leading to the driveway, her foot hard on the accelerator all at once wishing that the maximum speed of the bike was ninety instead of forty. She felt like flying!

She surrendered her moped to Lazslo, giving him a dazzling smile. When she saw his indulgent, tender look, she closed her eyes a moment. Oh Lord! How did he find out? Did Pendleton tell him? Did Mary? It seemed as though everyone knew but the father.

An idea so brilliant pierced her brain that she grabbed for the wrought iron railing as she ascended to their suite. She would tell Aaron to join her in her bath. Then while they were frolicking, in between all the festivities, she would tell him. She giggled out loud, making the housemaid goggle at her.

She stood in the bathroom for long moments, studying the array of jars, liquids, and powders that could be added to the water. She couldn't make up her mind. She couldn't make it too heavy. Aaron wouldn't like that. But he would like something elusive, exotic, sexy. She hummed to herself as wrinkled her nose at her discards, then finally ran the water and began lacing it with her choice of bath salts. She inhaled and was delighted, then looked at her watch. She had been in here twenty minutes.

She ran into the bedroom. The sight of Aaron buttoning the cuffs of a sea green silk leisure shirt brought her up short. "You have to have a bath," she wailed at him, waving a crystal flagon of Joy essence in his face. "It's ready."

Aaron studied her in the mirror, then turned slowly, his mouth stretching into a smile. "Your blouse is open to the waist. I hadn't realized how much of you was tanning."

Derry stared at his approach, mute, loving the way he looked in sea green silk trousers that fit his muscular legs like a second skin. The shirt had no fastenings except at the cuffs, which buttoned tight at the wrists. The gypsy sleeves were full, the shirt wrapping round his body and tying to one side. "Are you a descendant of Captain Frith as Lazslo is?" She was breathless.

"At this moment I feel like a buccaneer." His grin showed the dimples that so often of late had been hidden from her. "I think I'd like to bundle you in one of those drapes, toss you over my shoulder and kidnap you."

"Can't do that with sheer drapes; they have to be damask." She was out of breath. "You don't have a patch over one eye."

"I'll borrow Jim's." He kept coming; watching with absorbed interest as she fumbled with the buttons over her breasts.

"You don't have a ship. Can't do that on a Sunfish."

"I'll fake it," Aaron growled, reaching for her and pulling her close to him with a throaty chuckle. His mouth was a hard promise on hers.

With a sigh, Derry released her hold on the buttons, imagining herself and Aaron in the round marble tub. She realized that a tub was the farthest thing from Aaron's mind as his breathing hoarsened. "Wait," she whispered.

"Wait?" Aaron lifted his head, his eyes glassy. When Derry would have pulled back from him, he tightened his hold.

"Not to worry. You'll like it." She could feel her own pulse thumping in her ears as she took his hand and pulled him toward the bathroom. "This is just for us."

Aaron's puzzled frown softened as he followed her into the tiled room. He inhaled. "Ummm. Sexy. Is that for us?"

"It is. Like it?" Derry felt her smile slip sideways at the heat in his gaze when he looked at her.

"Oh yes, I like it, devil doll." Even as he spoke he was pushing the blouse off her shoulders again. His hands were agile yet gentle as he divested her, then himself of clothing.

He lifted her into his arms and stepped down into the tub, letting the bubbly wetness cover them both. "Ahhh," Aaron murmured. "The ultimate escape from my family: the bath."

"If Sylvie heard you now, she would tear a strip off your hide." Derry crooned to him, loving the floating sensation of her body against his.

"Open up your eyes, lotus flower," Aaron said to her, his hand massaging her skin.

"I don't know if I have the strength." Derry made an effort to raise her lids.

"You feel so good. I hope you know that we will be making love in here," he chuckled in her ear.

Derry's lids lifted part way. "Not a very original thought, since I had it first."

"You mean I'm being seduced?" Aaron snarled softly, his hands moving her over the top of his body.

"Any objections?" Derry felt like giving a Rebel yell, or Indian love call, or a plain old Yankee hoot.

"None. You will have my full cooperation, wife." Aaron's hand slid gently down her body finding the pulsing curves and caves that not only excited her, but heated him as well.

"Aaron . . . Aaron . . . ohhhh, don't do that . . . yes, do that . . . Aaron" She could feel herself breaking away, falling off the edge of the world. Vaguely she remembered she wanted to talk to him.

"Derry . . . darling . . ." Aaron lifted her body over him as his tongue ministered to her, the spasmodic reaction of her form having an erotic effect on him. "Your body is so sweet, so good."

"Aaron." Derry dug her hands into him, remembering how he had loved the feel of her fingers pressing into his flesh. It became of paramount importance to her that she give this man more pleasure than he had ever had before this moment. Everything else left her head as her mind and body opened to Aaron. Even if she wanted to control the cascade of emotion she doubted that she could.

The swell of passion engulfed them for long moments, its ebb like a long, sweet sigh of relief.

"I have to get you out of here, love." Aaron rose, like a dolphin from the bubbling water, his strong arms lifting her with him. "You have lovely recreational ideas, lady," he mumbled into her ear as he cocooned her in a heated bath sheet.

"Thank you, kind sir." Derry slurred her words as she rested sleepily on Aaron while he dried her.

"I think it's time you had a short nap." Aaron chuckled, lifting her as she yawned.

"No time. Company." She tried to lock her jaws against another yawn and failed.

"We have time. Telford will watch the children."

"Thank God for Telford," Derry murmured as she cuddled up to her husband's bare chest as he lay beside her.

Derry woke with a feeling of urgency, of need. The children! Aaron's family!

The arm around her middle tightened. "Don't get tense," Aaron muttered, his fingers splaying on her thigh.

"We should get ready." Derry felt the strain dissipating as Aaron stroked her. "I really must get up." Regret filled her voice.

"All right." Aaron whisked out of bed, pulling her with him, making her laugh.

"When you move, you really move." Derry felt the warmth of his hands as he slipped a silken wrap around her body.

"Good service. That's my motto."

Her mouth dried up as she looked at his bronzed, naked form. He was beautiful! She watched him as he dressed and then, unable to restrain herself, flung her arms about him.

The door leading to the hall flew open. "Well, really, Aaron, you might have come down to meet Delia and me. We've brought the children."

Aaron sheltered Derry with his body, his frame now rigid with fury. "Get out of here, Blane. I mean it. How dare you come to our private apartments!"

Derry could feel the pumping of angry blood through his system as he cradled her to his body. She didn't even bother to peep over Aaron's shoulder to see her sister-in-law. She could imagine the tall, aristocratic Blane, her high planed, patrician features pinched in disgust.

His sister sniffed. "I hope you will not continue to show discourtesy to—"

"Get out." Aaron snarled, releasing Derry and whirling around to face his sister.

The door slammed behind Blane. Aaron took in a shuddering breath of air before he faced Derry.

"I can see why you would find our life together intolerable, why you ran from me, divorced me." He bit off the words and spat them into the room. His agate hard eyes took on an introspective look. "I don't know why I didn't see it more clearly." His jaw seemed hewn from granite. "But I certainly will set the whole damn lot of them straight." Without another word to her, he left the room, the door slamming again.

"The Lathrops love to bang doors." Derry sighed,

stretching, still feeling the euphoric ache of their lovemaking. She glanced at the gold clock sitting on the dresser and yelped, stripping off the silken wrap as she rushed to the bathroom.

After she applied her makeup and donned the apricot-colored lingerie that she favored along with the sheerest of hose, she turned to the clothes caddy to see what had been hung there for her to wear. She had to smile at the choice. The dress was in teal blue silk, almost the shade Bermudians call Bermuda blue. The strapless sarong touched her knee, the opening at the front opening to mid-thigh.

She wrapped it around her body, knowing that her convex tummy would show. Derry smiled at her reflection, feeling pleased with herself as she placed both hands on her abdomen. It wasn't until she looked upward at herself that she was aware that her burgeoning breasts were rather too prominent. It surprised her a bit since she had always considered herself a small busted woman. "You'll really set Delia and Blane on their aristocratic derrieres if you go down wearing this sarong," she mused, pointing to her mirror image. She turned this way and that. It was a little more daring than anything she would have worn when she and Aaron were married the first time. She always tried to find the most demure garment that she could for any of the family's performances.

"So what?" She shrugged at the mirror.

She inhaled deeply of the soft air coming through the windows. She gazed out over the sky blue water, feeling her spine stiffen. "My job is to be a good wife to Aaron and a good mother to our children," she pronounced out loud, her hands again going to her middle. "There are no other priorities before those." With that little pep talk behind her, she glanced once more at the clock and left the room.

She hesitated in the hallway, wondering if perhaps Telford still had the children upstairs. She shook her head at such a notion, sure that they had been downstairs for some time.

A frisson of worry slithered down her spine. Could she protect the children from . . . from what? Derry took a deep breath, giving herself a mental shake as she paused before descending the stairs. She paused again in the lower hall, taking deep breaths. She could hear the rise and fall of voices coming from the lanai and the lounge. Taking a deep breath and pushing it out her lips with a whoosh of air that lifted the damp tendrils on her forehead, she descended the stairs and entered the lounge. She looked right into her father-in-law's eyes. He winked.

"She's done it again Pendleton." Mother Lathrop announced *sotto voce,* but the words echoed in the sudden stillness. "I always raised our girls to greet their guests and not be late."

"And not much else. I wish you had taught them to be the lady that Derry is," Pendleton said in a conversational manner, ignoring the gasps of his wife, daughters, sister, and niece and going toward Derry with his hands outstretched. "How lovely you look, child." He kissed her cheek. "That special mother-to-be glow is showing," he whispered in her ear, before turning, pulling her hand through his arm and facing his family.

Aaron came up to her but before he could reach her, Ern was there, a glass of champagne in his hand which he proffered.

"Your children are delightful, Derry." His smile was for her alone. "I wish they were mine."

"Well, they're not. They're mine," Aaron said elbowing the man aside.

"Aaron is getting as ill-mannered as Derry, I think." Delia sipped her champagne.

Derry spoke, her hand restraining Aaron as he leaned toward his sister. "I must apologize for being late, Delia, as well as not welcoming you to Windrift." Derry beamed down at her sister-in-law who sniffed in acceptance of the apology. "But you see,"—Derry saw that the children were on the lanai with Telford. "Aaron and I make love in the afternoon, and that often makes us late." She grinned when Delia began to cough as she swallowed her champagne the wrong way. Derry obliging gave her a whack on the back that almost sent her off the couch.

"Pendleton," Mrs. Lathrop managed to say. Color rose in her face when she noticed that her son and husband were holding onto each other and laughing. Ern Griswold was chuckling. Derry didn't even notice the glint in his eyes. She was too busy trying to keep the sudden dizziness from effecting her behavior. When she felt the hard arm around her waist, she leaned back, grateful for the familiar support.

Blane rose to her feet, jabbing a long cigarette into an ivory holder, the snap of the cigarette lighter sounding like a shot in the silence. "You are getting very amusing, Derry." She smiled her Radcliffe smile. "You are also getting a little heavy dear. I would do something about that if I were you."

"I shall . . . in about seven months." She felt Aaron's grip loosen then clench on her body. "We really don't care if it's a boy or girl, since this will be our fourth." She looked up into Aaron's face. His eyes stared blindly ahead; his skin was saffron-colored. "Do we, darling?"

"No," Aaron said in a raspy voice.

"If it's a boy, though," Derry saw Lee leading Sara

into the room, Kim behind them, "we would want him to be just like our older son, Lee." She smiled at the boy.

"Are we to have a baby?" Kim bubbled over. "Betsy Whitney thinks she has the only mother who is having a baby. She will just have twin cats when I tell her," Kim announced, using the newest school phrase for surprise, her smug look making Aaron come out of his daze and give a hard laugh.

"I may have twin cats myself," he muttered in Derry's ear.

"What shall we call it?" Lee looked up at his parents.

"Baby." Sara announced, putting her thumb in her mouth when Grandpa laughed and lifted her into his arms.

"If it is a boy . . ." Derry pretended to think but she had already made up her mind what the name would be for a boy. "I think . . . we think that the name 'Devon Pendleton Lathrop' would be a good name.

"And Cassandra Parker Lathrop if it's a girl. Isn't that right, darling?" The lazy heat in Aaron's voice put her pulse into overdrive.

"Yes." Derry gulped.

"I like it, Mom," Lee said, unaware that he had melted Derry's bones by calling her "Mom."

"Me, too." Kim looked thoughtful. "But I like the name Eufemia, too. That is a name in the book Miss Flecker is reading to us."

"Babies is nice." Sara patted her grandfather's cheek with a chubby hand. "I big girl."

"Those names belonged to our other parents, sir," Lee explained to his grandfather, coming to stand beside him.

"Yes, I know." Pendleton Lathrop cleared his throat, blinking his eyes as though he were clearing them of something.

"You are a bit late starting a family are you not?" Delia spoke, her hand hovering over the canapes that Lazslo was offering her.

"Are you deaf or stupid or both, Delia?" Pendleton asked, taking his offspring by surprise. "This is Derry's fourth child." He looked at each member of his family in turn, including the husbands of Delia and Blane who had thus far been mute. He stared longest at his wife, who had her mouth open to speak; and to his sister, whose cheeks quivered. "And of course that is how the Lathrop family will look on this child . . . as the fourth child of Derry and Aaron. I shall be returning to Bermuda if the birth is to take place here."

Aaron stared at his father's inquiring look. "Uh . . . well we might be back in Laneport by then, but I don't know. Either way, father, you will be informed and invited to stay with us."

"Thank you, son."

"Congratulations to you both." Ern Griswold's smile had a twist to it.

Derry turned to smile at him, glad to look anywhere but at Aaron. "Thank you."

Ern bent to kiss her lightly on the mouth, his lips then sliding across her cheek to her ear. "I'm very envious of Aaron. I wish it was my child you were carrying," he whispered, his voice having a caressing lilt to it.

Derry pulled back to stare at him, then she felt herself lifted backwards, familiar hard arms around her waist.

"Derry and I thank you for your best wishes." Aaron's voice was stilted.

She twisted her head around to look at Aaron's face, but she could read nothing on that closed, shuttered facade.

"I . . . ah . . ." Mother Lathrop shot quick looks at her husband as though she were trying to keep a tarantula at bay. "I think it would be nice if Derry came to Boston to have the baby. Aaron was born in—"

"Derry and Aaron will decide where their child is to be born, then they will inform us." Pendleton stated in low tones.

"Of course." Mother Lathrop looked at her sister-in-law, Sylvie, who was staring in a fixed way at her brother.

"You seem to be going through some dreadful change of life, Pendleton," Sylvie drawled.

"Oh, is that what it is? No matter. I've just decided that I will have the only say in my household, no matter which one, and I will handle the finances personally henceforth."

"What are you saying, Pendleton?"

Pendleton Lathrop seemed to turn to ice. "What do you think I am saying, Sylvie?"

"Are you trying to curtail my share of the Lathrop money because of some misguided idea that you—"

"Quiet!" Pendleton raised his voice a fraction, causing Lee to stare at him.

Sylvie inhaled, seeming to swell. "If you think that I will stand still for you cutting me out of my share of the Lathrop money—"

"What share? What you inherited, you spent. Since then you have been relying on the foolishness of my wife—"

"Pendleton!" His wife's eyes were straining from her head.

"—and the softheadedness of me." Pendleton's head swung to include Donald, his sister, and his daughters and their husbands. "The free ride is over. Depend on your own resources henceforth." He looked back at his sister. "And you, Sylvie, can live on Peabody's money, not mine. Make do, Sylvie. Everyone else does. So remember, the next time you wish to travel with your children to Bermuda or anyplace else, you will pay your own way."

Donald let out a strangled moan about getting employment.

"From now on," Mr. Lathrop continued, chucking Kim under the chin, "my money will be channeled where I want it to be . . . to *whomever* I want it to be." He smiled at Kim, Lee, and Sara, while the buzz of fury rose in the room.

Derry stepped closer to her father-in-law when the furor abated. "Pen." She coughed, realizing she had never before spoken when the Lathrops were "discussing" their family business. "I don't know what you plan to do with your money, but I won't let you spoil the children by giving them too much."

Over the sounds of "What a nerve" from Donald and Mother Lathrop's "Well, I never," Aaron spoke.

"Derry and I are in agreement on how the children should be raised." He smiled at his father and glowered at the rest of his family until the disgruntled mutters died away.

"My boy, I promise that I will do nothing that would displease you or Derry." He bent to put a wriggling Sara on the floor with Kim and Lee.

When he straightened, he looked right at Derry. "One of the first things I would like to do, now that the children's summer vacation has begun, is take them back to Laneport. Jim and Barrow can help us open up the house there. That would give you and Aaron the chance to stay here by yourselves for a while."

Ten

Derry knew she would miss the children, and she did, but there was a certain exhilaration in being alone with Aaron. For the last hour they had been together in the house, and she just realized that since her announcement of her pregnancy to the family a week ago, Aaron had managed to avoid being alone with her. For the first two nights she had tried to stay awake when he came to bed so that they could talk but she had been unable to keep her eyes open. Aaron was always gone before she woke up in the morning. Now, except for Lazslo and the staff that came daily, they were by themselves. Derry took a deep breath and expelled it. Did Aaron intend to avoid her for the two weeks they would be here together?

Slapping her hand on the limestone balustrade of the terrace, she made a vow. No way was that big oaf going to avoid her for two weeks! She would ferret him out right now and tell him that.

Not even finishing the thought, she whirled from the terrace calling for Lazslo.

"Yes, Mrs. Derry?" The serene Bermudian glided from the depths of the house and smiled at her.

Arms akimbo, she glared at him. "All right. Where is he? Where does he hide? And don't you dare try to lie to me, Lazslo." She shook her index finger in his face.

A smile wreathed his chestnut-colored face. "I am most happy to tell you, my lady, that he is no doubt in the boathouse sanding the bottom of the skiff. I have a great fear that all our wooden boats will turn into sawdust under the ministrations of Mister Aaron." Laughter glinted in those chocolate eyes.

When Derry yanked on his arm and pulled him down to press a kiss on his cheek, it was the first time that she had ever seen the tall man discomfited. She could tell that even though his dignity was dented, he was not displeased. "Pack me a French picnic, Lazslo while I change." Despite his adjurations to go slowly Derry took the stairs two at a time to their suite, shrugging out of her skirt and blouse. It took mere minutes to don the turquoise micro bikini that barely covered her. She placed her hand on her rounding tummy that was in plain sight. "Shame on you, Mrs. Lathrop." She giggled. Then, after donning the thigh-length terry cloth robe in teal blue and slipping on the beach clogs, she descended the stairs.

An unruffled Lazslo stood in the hall holding out a deep wicker basket. "Madame, while you are at the boathouse, you should have Mr. Aaron show you the apartment. It was refurbished just before Sir Rupert's demise and is kept clean and . . . ready for use." His face was wooden, and he held the door open, looking just above her head. "There is brie, fruit, bread, and champagne."

"Thank you, friend." Derry went down to the drive, looking for her moped.

"It's been put away, Mrs. Derry, at Mr. Aaron's orders until after your baby is born. I can take you Ma'am, or you must walk." Lazslo spoke in firm tones.

Derry knew she wouldn't be able to change his mind. "I'll walk."

The walk was lovely, and she stopped often to sniff a flower or watch a bird. She felt a fluttering of unease as she approached the pink stucco building that matched the main house. She stepped onto the wooden bridge that led to the second story of the building. The second story was on the street level and led directly into the apartment that Lazslo mentioned. Derry skirted the building until she came to the stairs that led to the boat and water level. She peered into the window of the door and saw Aaron bent over the upside down sail boat, his hands pushing in rhythmic motion along the surface. She took a breath and pushed open the door. "Hi."

Aaron raised his head from his work, his look flat and closed to her. "Hi."

"I've brought food for us."

"Just leave mine there. I'll get it later." Aaron motioned with his head.

"The hell I will." Derry banged the innocent wicker basket down on a board suspended between two horses. Jamming her fists on her hips, she glared at him. "Either you go swimming with me or I fly back to the mainland." She could feel her jaw thrusting forward.

The cast iron look to Aaron's features could crack a hair.

"Just like that. You'd take off on me again." His words sounded harsh.

"No. I'm not leaving you, but I won't be ignored,

and you act as though you don't want me around you."

His throat worked as though golf balls were trying to get down his throat. "I want you around me. I always have, but . . . when I'm with you I want to make love to you, and now you're pregnant, and I don't want anything to happen to you."

Relief filled her body like helium. She threw off her towelling robe watching his eyes rivet to her body. "Is that all? Fool. The doctor told me I'm right as rain. I'm gaining weight—"

"Yes you are." He muttered, his hand coming out to touch her as though he couldn't control the action. His fingers feathered her stomach, the touch tender, almost reverent. "Your tummy is so round." His voice was low and hoarse.

"It's supposed to be." She felt filled with pride in her body under Aaron's look. "You'll probably hate me when I'm big as a house." She didn't believe it for a minute.

"No." Aaron groaned his other hand coming out to touch her skin. "You'll be even more beautiful than you are now, if that's possible." His eyes lifted to her face, the liquid emerald look warming her as nothing else could ever do. "You are one beautiful woman, devil doll."

Breathless, Derry laughed up at him and moved one step closer to him, bringing his hand flat to her body. "Do you like it that you are going to be a daddy . . . again?"

"Yes." His eyes wandered over her body again. "But I would like it with you with no children, even though it doesn't seem possible that we never had children before now." He laughed briefly, his body bowing over hers, the hand at her waist slipping to her back. "I have the feeling sometimes that you really did give birth to Lee and Kim and the baby."

"Not baby. Big girl." Derry imitated Sara, lifting her hand to pat his cheek as the little girl often did.

Aaron took a deep breath and pulled her closer, then released her as abruptly. "I'm dirty and sweaty from working."

"Then let's take a swim." Derry took another step forward, feeling an aggressive confidence alien to her.

"I'm damned glad we have a private beach. Too much of your breasts show in that skimpy top," he breathed, his mouth dropping to the velvet flesh pushing up from the bikini top. "Far too much." Aaron pushed back from her and unbuckled his faded, paint-smeared cutoff jeans, showing the black swim briefs. He took her hand and led her back out onto the deck, then down the steps to the water and the beach. Their cove was very private, the horseshoe shape making a protected area for bathers or sailors of small crafts.

Instead of running into the water as she had planned to do, Derry felt the earth swing away as Aaron lifted her into his arms and carried her into the surf.

He lowered her into the water gently, using his body as a shield as he did so.

She paddled on the top of him until the breath-catching first moments subsided and she was able to strike out on her own. She had been swimming for several minutes when she heard Aaron call out and point. She followed his direction and saw the dreaded low mounds that pinpointed the Portuguese man o' war. The waves were bringing them in fast as Derry turned away from them. It wasn't until she was close to shore that she saw that some of the creatures were between her and the

sand. She looked around her and saw that she
was hemmed by them. She took a deep breath
hoping to throw herself under them, when all at
once Aaron was there, sweeping her high into his
arms and splashing through them. She saw him
wince and mutter. "Damn things."

On the beach Derry struggled to be let down so
that she could look at his legs. She only saw two
of the ugly stings but she was sure she remembered that they were poison.

"Not to worry, darling. Lazslo keeps a lotion up
in the apartment just for this. No danger. I mean
it."

Derry followed close on his heels, noting the
swelling around the stings. She tried to hover
over Aaron while he medicated himself, but he
went into the bathroom and shut the door. "If
you're not out of there in two minutes, I'm coming in to get you," she muttered to the closed
door.

He was out in one minute, smiling at her.

She held him still while she peered at the stings.
They did look better. "If you get one smidgeon of
fever we go to the doctor. Agreed?" Derry geared
herself for battle.

Aaron opened his mouth, then grinned at her
mulish look. "Agreed, boss."

"I'll go down and get the basket." She turned
away.

"No." He put two strong hands on her waist.
"I'll get the basket. You set the table in the bow
window."

Derry was enchanted with the new treatment of
the window that reached from ceiling to floor, the
two side panels open to catch the ocean breeze,
the tied-back white sheers having a dotted Swiss
pattern. Instead of a centerpiece of flowers, there
was a basket of ivy hanging low in front of the

center panel of the bow window. She found an Irish linen cover in the teakwood highboy and napkins of the same material.

When Aaron returned she was just putting white candles into crystal holders. She grinned at him. "Even if we don't light them they will be pretty."

"We'll light them." Aaron pronounced, staring at her. "Though how I'm supposed to eat with you dressed like that I don't know."

"Oh, I'm going to shower before I eat." Derry looked down at the salt-flecked bikini.

"You have clothes to change into?"

Derry's mouth dropped open, making Aaron laugh. "I forgot."

"That's all right, love. I must have an old shirt that you can borrow after we shower."

She nodded, suddenly shy of him as she saw the old, confident Aaron stroll toward her.

"I'm going to scrub the salt from your skin," he mouthed into her neck, lifting her into his arms.

"Salt is very drying to skin." Derry swallowed.

"True." He let her slide down his body in the bathroom, but he didn't release her even as he adjusted the shower head and water.

"This is a much smaller shower unit than in our suite," Derry stated as he loosened her top and threw it toward the wall of the bathroom. "You're not very neat."

"True." He rolled the skimpy bottom down her legs, pausing to kiss each knee cap. His hand cupped her buttocks as he urged her to step out of the briefs. "Your skin tastes salty. But good," he observed, making his way back up her form with his mouth.

"Of course," She answered breathlessly.

"Derry, I love you. I wanted our first marriage to last, and I'm determined that nothing will come between us again."

"I'm surprised that you didn't have Ern Griswold as your best man the second time," she said, vaguely remembering saying the same thing before.

"No," he said testily, lifting her into the warm spray of water. "He wants you. He's wanted you from the moment he met you at the luncheon Sandy had for us."

"You mean the one where your sisters sat isolated from everyone?"

He frowned down at her naked body. "I saw him watching you, and I could smell danger. All I wanted to do was pick you up and run out of there."

"Is that why you seemed so aloof to me?"

"I wasn't aloof, love," Aaron protested, wrapping her in a fresh towel. "I guess we need to have this talk and then take a shower. Right?"

"Right." Derry swallowed. "I thought you were having doubts about marrying me that day. I was scared." She reached up to stroke the cheek that had the beginnings of bristle.

"God. I wasn't having second thoughts about marrying you. I was just trying to keep from murdering Ern. Every time I turned around, he was close to you, laughing with you, teasing you." He settled her on his lap when he sat down on the loveseat in the bedroom of the apartment.

"Your sisters kept bringing Ern over to me," Derry said, her voice measured as she recalled the other times during her courtship and marriage that Delia and Blane would have Ern in tow when they met her for lunch.

"I see now that it was a deliberate wedge in our marriage." Aaron gnashed his teeth.

"They would invite me places and bring Ern with them." Derry felt an angry grief. "Why wasn't I smart enough to see what they were doing?" She looked up at Aaron. "I never thought of Ern as anything but your friend . . . and a friendly face in the hostile Lathrop camp. I never understood why you questioned me so much about him."

"Whenever he was in our company I saw him watching you, eating you up." Aaron's throat worked as though he was swallowing a large cotton ball. "I wanted to kill him. I was afraid of losing you. He still wants you, the way he's wanted you from the beginning." He cradled her towel-wrapped body to him. "He can't have you. No one can."

"You're crazy, do you know that?" Derry reached up, scoring his cheek with one nail. "Ern has been your friend since Choate. You told me that."

"No one is my friend who wants you. His eyes still follow you. I only felt relief when he left with the family." He looked down at her, his eyes fixed to her face. "Do you deny that he tried to move in on you after the divorce?" Aaron's face worked as though the bones were trying to escape through the skin, yet his hands on her body were gentle and sure.

"Don't be silly. I certainly do deny it." Derry began, exasperated with him. Then she remembered the phone calls. Ern had called her several times, she had thought to talk as a friend, but he had mentioned that he would like to come to Laneport to take her out to dinner. She had scratched that, knowing that the sight of Aaron's friend would be like sticking a hot poker in a fresh wound. She had demurred, not considering that Ern would want to see her other than to commiserate with her. "I didn't think of it that way," she murmured under her breath, feeling his arms tighten on her body.

"He did get in touch with you, didn't he?" Aaron's voice was velvet steel.

"Yes."

"And he wanted to see you didn't he?"

"Yes."

Aaron inhaled a deep breath, his chest swelling under Derry's cheek. "I could tell when I met him, from time to time, that he had spoken to you. I wanted to kill him, and I would have if he had tried to get close to you."

"Darling, don't . . ." Derry could feel her throat clot with tears as she felt his body flex with pain.

"Losing you, being divorced from you, was the worst thing that had ever happened to me."

"Me, too. Me, too." She choked, her hands clenching on his body.

"Those first months, I didn't care what happened." Aaron's laugh was hard. "The funny thing was that the drunker I became, the more my family blamed it on you." His arms gripped so hard she felt numb. "Why didn't I see then what they had done to us?"

Derry kissed his lightly stubbled chin. "I didn't know how to reach you . . . I mean get through to you . . . when I heard about your drinking. I guess I was afraid I would do more harm by talking to you . . ." She stammered, her words rushing over each other, the black thoughts she was sure were interred in the recesses of her mind surfacing like a geyser. "I wanted to call you, make you stop drinking. Ern told me what you were—"

"How often did he call?" Aaron asked hoarsely.

"Huh?" Derry blinked up at him, diverted from her train of thought by the question. "I don't know. Now and then." She pulled his head down. "I didn't care how often he called as long as he would tell me about you. I was sick when he told me about your drinking. It frightened me so much. I used to pace the floor at night, unable to sleep."

"I never slept." Aaron pronounced in flat tones. "Not from the time you left me. I drank, hoping I'd pass out. A couple of times I did." When Derry gasped he hugged her close to him. "I shouldn't tell you this."

"Yes you should. I want us to tell everything to each other." She felt an unaccustomed wetness on her cheeks. "No more secrets, no more hiding from each other."

"Never again, my love." His lips closed over hers in gentle fierceness.

Derry could feel a surge of confidence flow through her, a strength of purpose, an awareness of the powerful, positive psychology of love. Love makes superwomen of us all, she mused in giddy wonder.

Derry closed her eyes, loving the massage of his hands as he removed the towel. She reached up to finger the crisp hair at his neck. "I didn't want to divorce you, my love. I did it in self defense. I was frightened . . . so afraid that you would be contemptuous of me after a while, that you would begin to echo your family's opinion of me."

He looked down at her, a half smile on his face as one of his fingers traced her upper body. "You were perfection to me. That's what my family knew and what you didn't know. I would never have listened to one word they said against you. They knew that. That's why they used a different tactic." His smile had a self derisory glint to it. "They knew where I was most vulnerable with you. I was jealous of you."

"That's what Pen said." Derry whispered.

"My father is a quiet man, and damned smart." He looked past her, as though he would study the tiles on the wall. "They took every opportunity to tell me how many times you saw Ern when I was in England, or Beirut, or Peking. Finally they didn't even have to tell me anything anymore. My imagination took over the moment we were apart. God,

Derry, I'd wake up in a cold sweat after a night-mare where Ern was making love to you."

"Aaron." She closed her hands on each side of his face. "Not once from the time we met, did I ever think of another man in a sexual way, not even Gerard."

"You were going to marry him." Aaron scowled.

"We talked about this before," she reminded him, feeling happy to be so close to him. "But, as I was saying, even with Gerard . . . I–I guess I just blanked out the thought of him making love to me."

"Don't talk about that." Aaron spoke through clenched teeth.

". . . or even touching me." She finished in soothing tones. "There has never been anyone for me but you, Aaron. I love you desperately." She tried to grin, but she felt her face collapse with feeling.

Aaron's breath jerked out of his body as his mouth forayed over her face, touching each pore. "I feel weak as a kitten, but strong enough to lift up the island of Bermuda with one hand."

"Don't do it." Derry chuckled. "Bermudians are very good-natured but I don't think they would like anyone roughhousing their island." She was warm, secure, loved. "No one will be able to wedge us apart again. Not your family, not anyone."

Aaron shook his head. "Nothing can ever touch us, devil doll. For the first time, during their visit, it sank in what you must have gone through with them, what they had done to you." He lifted her up his body with both hands cupped on her back-side. "Almost from their arrival I began to see how shallow they can be, how facile their priorities. But when Sylvie had the gall to say she had in-vited Ern Griswold to our home, I realized that

they were being deliberately obstructive and de-
structive to our marriage. I could cheerfully have
thrown the lot of them in St. George's Bay." Aaron
reached for another warming bath sheet.

"Not another one." Derry gasped, laughing.
"We're having warm weather, not blizzards.

Aaron ignored her, wrapping her like a mummy
before tying a towel around his waist. "You're a
mother-to-be. You have to be cosseted . . . by me."

"I can't move." She smiled up at him, raising
her eyebrows as she saw the gathering frown on
Aaron's face. "What is it?"

"I almost fainted when you announced we were
going to have a baby. I actually saw stars for a
second. Wouldn't that have been something if I
passed out then? Stop laughing. It wasn't funny.
You're not supposed to announce a man's upcom-
ing fatherhood with a blithe general announcement. I might have had a heart attack." He
had a hurt look on his face when Derry laughed
helplessly.

"You're a father of three. You should be an old
hand." Derry giggled.

"Very funny. It didn't help. My hands were shaking." He had a faraway look in his eye. "I'm going
to sign up for that LaLeche course."

"Honey, that's for women who want to breast-
feed." Derry hiccupped, still laughing.

"Oh. Are we going to do that?" Aaron's eyes
gleamed with interest.

"*I* am." She tried to look solemn. "I don't think
you qualify."

"Be serious, Derry. This is important."

She looked up at him, feeling the smile on her
face broaden, not bothering to hide the feelings
that she knew would be showing on her face. She
studied his every pore, the tiny scar at the bridge

of his nose, the whitish one on his chin. "You were a harum scarum boy. I can tell by the marks on your face."

"Yes, my darling one, I was." He bent to lift her high in his arms. "I was the wild one. My mother disowned me every other day. One of the best things that ever happened to me was being sent away to school at an early age."

"Your mother would have suffocated you."

"Fortunately, she disliked little children, so I escaped quite a few close calls like ballroom dancing and gentleman's etiquette class."

"Do they really have such things in this century?" Derry inquired.

Aaron nodded. "Donald attended. But when I threatened to loosen all Donald's teeth if I had to go to the class, my mother backed down." Aaron grinned at her.

Derry didn't say that she could finally see behind the tough facade that Aaron always presented to the world to the young, frightened boy who must have felt unloved much of the time. "Your father was away a great deal, wasn't he?"

"Yes. First for the State Department, then for the World Bank. I was proud of him."

"And so you should be," Derry murmured, thinking how lonely Aaron must have been when his father was away. She pushed even closer to him.

He obliged her by holding her even closer, his chin on her hair. "I didn't see father much, really, until after we married. He often talked to me about you. He encouraged me to try and rebuild our life together."

"I didn't know that," Derry whispered.

"Yes. He told me that what we had together was too precious to throw away without a fight." Aaron leaned back, his voice deepening and sounding much like his father's. "A Lathrop fights for what he wants."

"That even sounds like him." She nibbled on Aaron's chin. "He loves you, Aaron. We had long talks together and he regrets not being there when you needed him."

"I've always known that my father wanted what was best for me. Naturally he would know that was you and the children."

"He loves Lee, Kim, and Sara. And they love him."

"Sara wraps him up like a package every time she smiles at him." Aaron smiled down at her. "He also seems to love his daughter-in-law." Aaron lifted her into his arms and carried her through to the bedroom, unwrapping her from the second towel and putting her gently between the silken sheets. He took a deep breath as he lay down beside her, his hands going to her body, his mouth moving over her navel, the tenderness making her flesh quiver. "Do you really love me, Derry?" Aaron lifted himself to look down at her. It was all there, the skin and bones peeled back, the inner man exposed, raw, waiting.

Surprise riddled her. "Of course I love you. I have always loved you. You know that."

"I need to hear you say it." His throat moved as though a rock was being dislodged there, the spasm rising to his face, cheekbones clenching, forehead wreathed with strain. "I wanted to know that for a reason, devil doll. Having you love me completes me, puts the last puzzle piece of my life in place. You're the steel in my spine, the softness in my soul, the music in my heart. You make my brain function, my legs walk, my teeth chew." The lopsided smile touched her like a brand. "Everything in life came easy to me but you. There were easy barriers to any hurt or pain but not to you. I could armor myself for any spear thrust but yours. Any obstacle was just a good jump until you." The smile faded, then fluttered back. "Now there's surrender."

Derry chuckled, grasping his neck with both hands and pulling him down to her again. "Arrogant man! Darned mind reader! How did you know that all I ever wanted to do was to surrender to you." She nipped his chin with her teeth, laughing. "Damn your eyes for reading me like a book."

"All wrong, devil doll."

Derry stared at him, puzzled.

"You don't know what I'm saying do you?"

"I guess not." Derry felt a strange flutter in her chest.

"I wasn't talking about your surrender, devil doll." He muttered into her neck, his body covering hers with gentle possessiveness. "I was speaking of mine. *My* surrender to you, my love. Totally and unconditionally to you, Derry." He swallowed. "You have the power to hurt me, lady, hurt me so badly that I feel more dead than alive, but I'm yours just the same."

Tears slid from the corners of her eyes, her lips trembling as she held him close to her. "Oh darling, darling Aaron. I love you like that. I do. I do." She clung to him, letting her hands move feather-like over his body. The taut outlines of his form were an erotic impetus to her body. She could feel the curl of want become a tangle of need in her lower abdomen as the response to him rose like a flood. "I need you, Aaron. I have always needed you."

Fire erupted between them, making their skin meld together. Hunger met hunger, need met need, love collided with love to ascend with leaping heat,

join, and descend with a boiling serenity that was
theirs alone.

"I'll always love this apartment." Derry breathed
into his chest, happiness bubbling in her. She
lifted her head as the thought struck her. "That
reminds me, Aaron. You never did tell me how
you were able to decorate Windrift so fast."

He pulled her down onto his chest, letting her
hair fan out upon him. "I had talked to Jim and
to my father too about doing the place over to
induce you to come back to me. I guess I must
have talked about doing it many times when I was
drunk, because it seemed that whenever I was
sober, either Jim or my father would urge me to
begin the renovation of Windrift." His face twisted, a muscle at the corner of his mouth moving
slightly. "I woke up one day in a hotel. I had no
memory of how I got there, or even of where I was
at first. Much of that time is a total blank to me."

"Darling." Derry trembled, experiencing fear as
she thought of him so alone.

He rubbed her arm absently. "I sat there, holding my head, realizing I would never have a chance
of getting you back if I didn't screw my head back
on." He exhaled. "I stopped drinking . . . cold. I
went to an architect friend of mine and told him
about the few structural changes that I wanted
made." He smiled at her. "It started the ball rolling. Jim and my father jumped at the chance to
help me. As I got stronger, I became more determined that nothing would keep you from me.
After the interior was finished I started on the
landscaping. The work was like therapy. I could
feel my strength of mind and body returning. I
took an interest in the business again. My spirits
were up. The last thing I did here was this apartment. The entire place was complete before I took

the job in Senegal. I guess that's why I didn't get the word about you and . . . Gerard." He dropped the name like a bomb.

Derry stroked him. "Tell me the rest."

"That's what I was coming to talk to you about that day when Lee had been in the fight with the boy Timmy." He watched her, a slash of red on his cheekbones. "You were so beautiful and so mad at Timmy's father. Even though we had had plenty of arguments I had never seen you take the gloves off like that before. I wanted you right then. I could have made love to you right there on the porch."

Derry gave a choked laugh. "What would Gerard have said?"

"That pompous ass came damned close to being dismembered." Aaron growled. "I couldn't believe it when he said that he was going to marry you. At first I planned on strangling him the moment the kids were out of the room. Then I cooled down a little and began to think things through. I could tell just by the new look about you that you weren't going to acquiesce to my wishes." He caressed her stomach. "Our baby is in there. I love that," Aaron mused.

"I love it, too, silly man, but you're digressing— in a most delightful way of course." Derry felt unfettered, floating free of the earth.

"Hm-m." Aaron grinned at her. "Ah, yes. That's when I began what I like to think of as 'The Master Plan,' or 'How To Get Derry Back As My Wife.'" He bent to rub his lips against hers. "There was never any danger of you being married to Gerard." His voice sunk to a growl. "No man was going to love you but me." A smile illuminated his face. "I knew enough about you to be sure that your emotions weren't involved with him."

"Arrogant, aren't you?"

"You said that before." He sobered. "I think the word 'desperate' describes me better at that time. My life was nothing without you. I knew that."

"There hadn't been anyone for me but you, before and after our marriage," Derry said in a soothing tone and then watched the play of emotions over his face.

He exhaled, letting his tongue trail down her body, laughing hoarsely when her body jerked in response. "I sensed that even without being in touch with you. I realize now that I would have always known if you had fallen in love with someone else."

"Not a chance," Derry crooned, massaging the taut muscles of his arms.

"I would need no telegram, no phone call, no cable to tell me if you loved someone else, Derry. My body would start to shrivel if that ever happened, my arms and legs would fall off." He grimaced down at her. "I'm talking pretty strange, I guess."

"No . . . no. That's the way I would feel. I used to block you out of my mind with work and more work. I couldn't think of you with another woman because that thought would have killed me." Derry leaned on him, finding the confessions they were making salubrious to her spirit, feeling the plaster of paris around her feelings breaking away as she came truly alive, truly open to the world around her. She could feel the tendons of her mind and spirit flex and stretch, her whole being yawned with relief as all the old fears dissipated through the chimney of her mind. All the cast iron reasons why she could not let herself love, give herself completely to Aaron, now softened like melting butter and floated away. "It's funny . . ."

"What's funny?" Aaron mumbled.

"Our marriage didn't break from the outside. What I mean is there were never other men or women that came between us."

"God, no," Aaron averred.

"Oh, you know what I mean. So many of the people we knew separated because one or the other found someone else. That wasn't the way it was with us. It was—"

"Chinese water torture," Aaron interrupted. "Or under another name, the family Lathrop. Oh don't look like that, devil doll. I'm not bitter about my family. I'm bitter about myself, that I should be so stupid, so thick . . ."

"Don't." Derry rubbed her tongue down his jaw-line, loving the feel of his body contracting under hers. "We're together now. we have a beautiful family. We're going to have another baby. We can be generous now—kind to ourselves, kind even to your family." She chortled. "I can't believe we're going to have four children."

Derry did believe it in several short months. She and Aaron had their lovely honeymoon, but both were glad to get back to Laneport and the children.

As Derry bloomed so did the interest of the children. The first time Sara felt the baby move, her eyes widened to frying pan size. She gaped toothily at her father.

"Baby go bump."

"No, no. Sara, that's the baby kicking," Kim said in her most grown-up voice.

Lee smiled at Derry. "The baby is feeling good, isn't he, Mom?"

Derry smiled at her children as they set the

table. She was sitting in the nursing rocker, the only place where her bulk was truly comfortable. Aaron was putting the finishing touches on the salad for dinner. "Yes. Dr. Blitz is very pleased with our baby."

"And with the mother?" Aaron asked, smiling easily, not quite masking the concern he felt.

"Mother is doing very well, even if she is a pound or two more than she should be." Derry laughed, determined to make Aaron as easy in mind about this birth as she was. He had attended every class in the prenatal clinic with her and had entered willingly into any and every course designed to give them information about the soon-to-be-born child.

That night, after the innumerable stories that were told on Derry's and Aaron's bed and all the school news had been hashed and rehashed, Kim and Lee were finally tucked in for the night. Sara had been asleep since shortly after supper.

Aaron came back to their room, watching her as she lay there, propped against three pillows. "Want me to rub some cocoa butter on your tummy?"

"Please." Derry's stretch marks on her tummy itched fiercely if Aaron didn't rub them with ointment.

As he ministered to her, he seemed to avoid looking at her.

"Darling? Aaron?" Derry quizzed, feeling cocooned and safe in the great love Aaron had for her. "Tell me what it is. You've been so quiet all week."

He looked up at her and smiled. "I'm fine." He tried to grin. "Hey, this man has a hard time being close to the woman he loves and not make love to her."

"Of course." Derry read the fear in his eyes. She wanted to tell him that all was well, but knew that if the shoe was on the other foot, she would be experiencing the same fear. When you love someone, it isn't easy, Derry thought, cradling his head to her as he held her body as though it were platinum. "Why is it when you love someone, you want to take away all the pain from them, all the danger?"

Aaron wouldn't look at her. He just shook his head.

He slept sitting up, holding her as he had been in the habit of doing since she had gotten too large to sleep supine.

When Derry awoke, she thought it was because she had a cramp in her leg that she sometimes got late at night. The pains in her back jarred her. She bit her lips to keep back any sound, thinking that they would fade and then she could sleep again.

After an hour she knew she was in labor, and though it was her first labor she sensed that it wasn't a false alarm. "Aaron. . . . Aaron."

Aaron called Linda Lisman to come and stay with the children and called the hospital to say that he was bringing Derry in.

"If it had only waited one day, your father would have been here to stay with the children." She tried to speak lightly and take deep breaths at the same time.

"Yes," Aaron barked, throwing quick glances at her as they sped through the night.

"Traffic is good," Derry said.

"It's generally light at three o'clock in the morning." Aaron answered her like an automaton.

When an attendant pushed a wheelchair toward Derry, Aaron scowled at him.

The attendant tried to explain. "Hospital policy is that the patient's are put into—"

"My policy is to carry my wife."

"Aaron," Derry began, torn between the pains that were coming closer together and the laughter at the bulldog look on his face.

All three—the doctor, Aaron and Derry—had mentioned that they expected the labor to be a prolonged one since this was Derry's first. All were prepared.

When Derry was changed into a hospital gown, she started the breathing exercises that would facilitate labor. Aaron's voice and arms held her, guided her, loved her.

"You're so beautiful, my love," he muttered to her.

"You must have a thing about baby whales then, because that's what I . . . ohhhh." Derry breathed through her mouth, increasing the take of oxygen.

"What is it?"

"Leave it to your child to want to rush everything. Ohhh, Aaron. . . . Hurry. . . . Call the doctor. . . . Ohhh. . . . This one is just like you, moving any and all obstacles out of the way. . . . Ohhh."

"Derry, darling." Aaron roared for the entire staff of the Upstate Medical Center to appear . . . on the trot.

Derry watched her son being born, and watched Aaron watch her. He didn't take his eyes off her the entire time it took to deliver the baby. He didn't hold the baby until he had bent over her. "I love you. I love you, wife of my heart."

When Devon Pendleton Lathrop came home, Kim, Lee, and Sara pronounced him just right for the family. Grandpa Lathrop said he hoped he would be as wonderful as the other three that were cuddled to his side.

That night, after the baby had been nursed and the house was quiet, Derry was happy to be cradled next to her husband's body once more. Aaron's body was home.

"Aaron? Do you remember on Bermuda when you said that you surrendered to me?"

"Yes I remember, and I meant it."

"I mean it too, my love, my husband. I surrender all of me, all my life to you." Derry felt the tears on Aaron's cheeks as he bent to kiss her.

THE EDITOR'S CORNER

The Editor's Corner is a continuing feature in our LOVESWEPT books. In months to come I'll be giving you information on our plans and tidbits on our authors. Now, though, in introducing our new line, let me tell you how excited we are about LOVESWEPT. And how proud we are to bring to you these fine love stories by some of the very best category romance writers in America! Talented storytellers are the centerpiece of LOVESWEPT. No gimmicks. No tired old formula books. Simply, extraordinary romances that will sometimes make you chuckle, sometimes bring a tear to your eyes, but always give you that warm, special feeling we trust you experienced from the story you've just finished. We think you will be very pleased that we're putting an end to the confusing use of pen names. Our authors are writing under their true names. You'll see each author's picture in her book and learn about her real life in her own words—who she is, how she feels about herself as a person and as a writer.

An interviewer asked me not long ago how I "dealt with all those prima donna authors." I was speechless; and the interviewer looked at me as though he were dealing with a moron. The reason I had no answer for a few moments was that not one of these talented women with whom I have the pleasure to work is even remotely like a prima donna! Each one is as delightful as the romances she writes. Truly, the LOVESWEPT authors make being an editor a joy!

(continued)

Some of the authors you'll encounter in this new line are seasoned pros. You know their work—under a variety of pen names—and you've shown through your purchases of their books that you love them. But you'll find, too, a lot of spanking new names. We are delighted by the fresh talent we've been able to discover and are publishing for the very first time.

And next month you are going to be treated to just such sparkling talent in Billie Green's A TRYST WITH MR. LINCOLN?, LOVESWEPT #7 . . . Helen Conrad's TEMPTATION'S STING, LOVESWEPT #8 . . . and Marie Michael's DECEMBER 32ND . . . AND ALWAYS, LOVESWEPT #9.

A TRYST WITH MR. LINCOLN? by Billie Green is filled with humorous surprises from the moment its heroine, Jiggs O'Malley, awakens in a strange hotel room (with one of the most devastating men I've had the pleasure to come across in paperback pages) . . . through an utterly sensual courtship . . . right until the exciting and heartwarming conclusion.

In **TEMPTATION'S STING,** Helen Conrad has made a lush Samoan island come alive. No piece of travelogue here, but a genuine portrayal of a South Pacific plantation in this day and age and owned by a man any woman would find difficult to turn down! Helen grew up on an island in the Pacific and certainly knows what she is writing about. I think that you're going to love Taylor Winfield's struggle to humanize the spoiled brat heroine Rachel Davidson. And what a delicious struggle it is!

DECEMBER 32ND ... AND ALWAYS by Marie Michael a story is just as intriguing as its title. Patrissa Hamilton thinks she's "over the hill" approaching her forty-first birthday. Never was there a man who could prove better than Marie Michael's hero Blaise, that a woman was not getting older; she was getting better.

I sincerely hope you've enjoyed these LOVESWEPT romances and will continue to enjoy them. I'm here, as our authors are, to bring you the best in romance reading. We count on two-way communication and welcome your comments and ideas.

With warm good wishes,

Carolyn Nichols

Carolyn Nichols
LOVESWEPT
Bantam Books, Inc.
666 Fifth Avenue
New York, NY 10103